ANTONIONI

series edited and designed by Ian Cameron

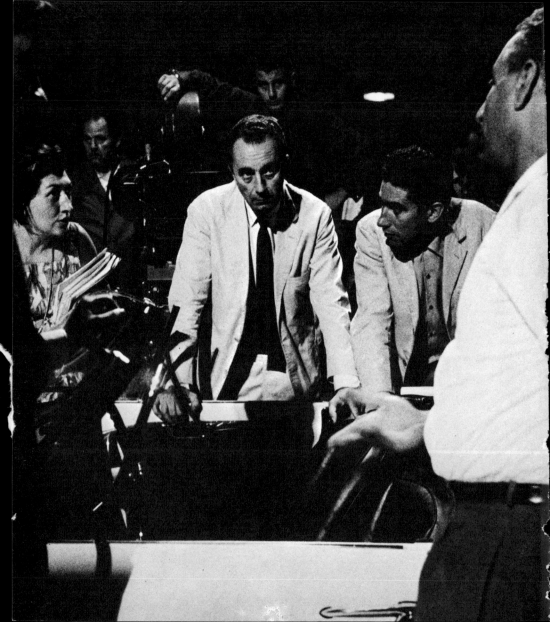

ANTONIONI

IAN CAMERON & ROBIN WOOD

PRAEGER

BOOKS THAT MATTER

*Published in the United States of America in
1969 by Frederick A. Praeger, Inc., Publishers
111 Fourth Avenue, New York, N.Y. 10003*

*Library of Congress Catalog Card Number:
72-91696*

Produced by Design Yearbook

Printed in England

CONTENTS

FOREWORD

The first part of this book was written during 1961 and the first half of 1962. Although it deals with all Antonioni's films up to *L'Eclisse*, it was initially undertaken because of the uninformed reactions which greeted *L'Avventura* on its arrival in Britain.

It seemed to me then—and still does—that the main value in Antonioni's work at that time lay more in what he did than in what he said. The misunderstanding of his films started with a lack of comprehension of his style, which was by no means as revolutionary as some commentators believed. Rather, in *L'Avventura* Antonioni was utilising the resources of the cinema to the fullest extent for one particular purpose. This was the demonstration of the feelings underlying human behaviour. It was in this area that Antonioni was least understood and it was here, rather than in the generalisations which he put forward, that his strength lay.

Antonioni was coming to grips with the problem of communicating to an audience the feelings of the characters without recourse to interior monologue when their spoken words rarely went further than providing clues. Eschewing the use of audience identification, he realised that evidence had to be presented of mental states, and this he provided with the utmost clarity. A director who, at the time, provided a useful comparison with Antonioni was Otto Preminger:

'In leaving us to notice actions and wonder about the motivation behind them, Preminger is demanding the same level of audience participation as Antonioni. There is a similar refusal to *explain* emotions to the audience. Both show us evidence and make us draw the conclusions. The difference is in aim. Antonioni is trying to *describe* the characters' emotions through their behaviour. He uses the camera to present the behaviour so that we will interpret it in a specific way, and be able to correlate our interpretations into a general conclusion. Preminger also presents us with evidence: words, voices, expressions, gestures, movement. But he does not tell us how to interpret it, either in the script or the direction—we have only the appearances to work on.

'As almost every action in the film [*Bonjour Tristesse*] is capable of at least two interpretations on the level of motivation, the audience must actively make choices rather than passively accept those of the director. Preminger's purposeful ambiguity contrasts with Antonioni's attempt at precise description.' (*Movie* 2)

The precision which informed every detail of the acting and camera-work was the great virtue of *L'Avventura*, an extremely unambiguous movie. The one mystery which remains unresolved—Anna's disappearance—stays that way because it does for the characters. The mystery is of where she went rather than why she went.

If spontaneity is sacrificed to clarity in *La Notte* and Antonioni is insufficiently aware of the neurotic nature of the heroine of *L'Eclisse*, both these films seem to me preferable to *Deserto Rosso*, where the generalisations which had been the weakest aspect of its predecessors became more crucial and where behavioural ambiguities abounded which the director seemed ill-equipped to handle. There is also the matter of the grey apples and the white rubber plant, which to me seem risible before they have a chance to be meaningful. Such details, though, are only symptoms of a general lack of sympathy which I feel for *Deserto Rosso* and *Blow-Up*. The films in colour are therefore the territory of Robin Wood, whose contribution to this book opens with an assessment of the later black and white films which largely treads the common ground between us.

I.A.C.

BLACK & WHITE FILMS

Cannes, 1962. The most eagerly awaited film of the Festival is Antonioni's *L'Eclisse*. Although it is the middle of a sunny May morning, the huge Palais des Festivals is half full for it. The evening show has long since been sold out. Antonioni himself is in hiding somewhere on the edge of town, and has only come to Cannes to give a press conference with Pietro Germi on their reasons for not coming to the Festival itself.

Before *L'Eclisse*, the audience has to sit through yet another short on folk-dancing which leaves it nothing to do but work up an even keener anticipation of the master's latest offering. The curtains part to the sound of a Twist played *fortissimo* as the titles flash on a blank screen. The audience is wholeheartedly on Antonioni's side.

Two hours later there is hissing from the balcony, and the critics file out silently, desperately trying to think up something snappy to surprise their colleagues and later their readers. A few have decided that the Eclipse of the title is Antonioni's. The rest concede, with qualifications, that he has done it again. There is a certain unwillingness to hazard any opinions on what he has done, but anyone will tell you how well, or badly, he has done it.

Two years before, *L'Avventura* had suffered a similar fate (less anticipation, more hissing), and set Antonioni on the way to becoming Bergman's successor as number-one cult director. I, for one, had expected that 1962 would be the year that Cannes capitulated to Antonioni. At least two years of repetitively consistent praise in almost every serious film magazine and newspaper should have had some effect, at least on the critics. But no. Antonioni is little better understood now in English-speaking countries than he was when *L'Avventura* appeared.

It was easy then to see the reasons for the trouble: at the time Antonioni's films had been shown very little outside Italy and France. Only *Le Amiche* and *Il Grido* had appeared, and passed unnoticed, in Britain and the United States respectively.

Antonioni is not so much difficult as different. General knowledge of the cinema is likely to be of less use to the spectator coming for the first time to Antonioni than to almost any other director. Without being consciously obscure or using techniques which are new in themselves, he is very different in spirit from most of his contemporaries—particularly from other Italians. He sets out to make a film about emotions, and refuses to let his cast emote according to the extrovert traditions of Italian screen acting. That would be 'rhetoric', one of his dislikes.

He set *L'Avventura* in a society that most people would consider decadent, and alienated more of them by concentrating relentlessly on individuals rather than social problems. Worse still, he abandoned 'the lower and middle classes where lives are constricted by necessity, to concentrate on the idle rich who have the time to torture each other.'

And even the critics not infected by social realism were sorely tried. Here was a long film with so little story that on paper it looked inconsequential. A film whose technique was so closely moulded to its author's intentions that it required the closest concentration for every second of its length. *Sight and Sound* remarked that it would 'probably tax any audience in the world.' Helped by an inaccurate synopsis, some British critics even got the plot wrong. The column-filling way out from their incomprehension was to say how difficult/ experimental/revolutionary it was.

But any film by any decent director, whether Welles or Vigo, Hitchcock or Mizoguchi, is an experiment in expressing whatever is important to its author through the subject he chooses or is given. If *L'Avventura* is revolutionary, it follows a line of similar if smaller revolutions.

Certainly it is not revolutionary in its technical resources. All the devices which Antonioni uses have been used before, although rarely in such a rigorously meaningful way. He has removed a large proportion of the linking shots whose only value is to make the spectator comfortable, to carry him gently from one time or place to another. The film is pared down to what Antonioni considers necessary. Answering an interviewer who suggested that certain sequences in *La Notte* were the most important, he said: 'If I'm sure that one sequence is less important than another I cut it out.'

His aim is, in the first instance, the most precise possible description of behaviour and, through behaviour, of emotions, the 'interior drama.' Bresson, who is also concerned with 'interior drama,' seeks to reach it by suppressing all the externals. Antonioni on the other hand has realized that it is impossible to communicate the 'interior drama' directly without the intervention of exterior drama—action or behaviour or dialogue—the evidence through which we recognize emotion in others. Everything irrelevant to his aim has been whittled down to a minimum. In an interview he explained: 'I always try to manage so that each element of the image serves the narrative, serves to specify a particular psychological moment. An image is only essential if each square centimetre of that image is essential.'

The difficulty people have over Antonioni occurs, I think, right at the start with the images themselves. Therefore I shall concentrate in dealing with the black and white films on the interpretation of the action and images. The first section is devoted to *L'Avventura* because it is the most familiar of these films, and so provides the best source of examples to use in explaining his methods. It is also the film in which these methods were perfected, and in a way explains the preceding films as well as the later ones. He has himself suggested that he was not precisely aware of what he was trying to say in *Il Grido*, and that it only became clear to him after he had made *L'Avventura* and *La Notte*. The greater clarity of *L'Avventura* suggests that he had finally rationalized the methods that he had used intuitively in the previous films. It seems at any rate that the changes in Antonioni's style since *L'Avventura* have been more consciously thought out than those before it. I should add that intellect is in no way superior to intuition in a director.

L'AVVENTURA

The story of *L'Avventura* is extraordinarily simple—during a yacht cruise, a girl disappears on a lonely island; her girlfriend and her lover search for her and begin an unstable relationship. Structurally the film is remarkable for its almost complete lack of resolution—particularly in the case of Anna, who is, after all, one of the two leading characters in the first part of the film. Little explanation is given for her disappearance, and none at all of what she has done. A few hints are planted that she might have gone away (sounds from unseen motor boats) or committed suicide (a dissolve from Claudia calling her name to waves crashing between two rocks, and a cut from Claudia holding Anna's blouse to a stormy sea), but nothing more. When Antonioni was in London in 1960, he was asked what happened to Anna. He replied, 'I don't know. Someone told me that she committed suicide, but I don't believe it.' That sums up Antonioni's whole attitude to plots and construction in films. As he is concerned with exploring situations rather than with tailoring neat plots, Anna is of no further interest to him after she has broken with Sandro —whatever the means she has used—and so she does not reappear. In 1960, most other writers or directors would, I think, have brought her back at the end to give a 'neat' construction and a 'dramatic' resolution.

Antonioni has called the story 'a detective story back to front'. Like the two protagonists we lose interest in the search for Anna as our attention is diverted to Sandro's affair with Claudia. Our experience of the events parallels the characters' experience in the film. We are never put in the position of knowing more facts than Claudia and Sandro. Because they never find out what happened to Anna, the director does not tell the audience.

We receive information as it is presented to the characters, in the wrong, or rather 'illogical', order. Example: we are not actually told until near the end of the film, when she mentions it to Patrizia, that Claudia comes from a poor family. In retrospect one can find sufficient evidence of her social position earlier in the film, but one realizes its significance only after one has been told—Antonioni relies heavily on the audience's power of recollection. The jumbled order in which we receive facts and the elimination of what Antonioni calls 'unnecessary technical baggage, . . . logical narrative transitions' are motivated by his belief that 'cinema today should be tied to the truth rather than to logic'. In life one does not get to know people in a logical way, and he does not see any reason for making things easy for his audience by changing this in his films.

Similarly, the length of each scene is dictated by the time it would take to happen. Antonioni avoids the sort of unreal screen time where crafty cutting is used to speed up the 'slow' bits of the action. If it takes a character ten seconds to walk across a courtyard, he will take ten seconds on the screen in *L'Avventura*, even though there is a cut from one camera position to another in the middle. Others might remove a second or two at the cut to prevent the film from dragging. But to Antonioni these seconds are just as important as the ones on either side. He subjects his audiences to real time as his characters would experience it: he would not sacrifice that to maintain a 'good' (i.e., brisk or at least steady) pace.

Although our experience may parallel that of the protagonists, we are not invited to identify with them. The method of acting and filming

is designed positively to discourage it. In place of subjective camerawork Antonioni favours deep not-quite-subjective shots with the camera close behind one of the characters who is visible in the frame. We observe more or less from his viewpoint without being sold the idea that we are looking through his eyes. In the earlier films, intimate scenes were normally shown in straight two-shot, which automatically places the camera even further outside the action as an observer.

Still: Sandro (Gabriele Ferzetti) greets Anna (Lea Massari) and Claudia (Monica Vitti).

The method of *L'Avventura* still does not allow identification, but involves the camera more closely with the action.

As we are shown what the characters see and learn, what they learn without identifying with them, our appreciation of their feelings must be primarily intellectual. We are therefore more conscious than the characters of the meaning of their behaviour (as we would not be if we started identifying with them). This places us in a position to correlate our observations of all the characters and reach the general conclusions which Antonioni expects us to draw.

Antonioni's concern with behaviour rather than story-telling shows in the treatment of the minor characters. Apart from Claudia, Anna, and Sandro, only Ettore, the architect for whom Sandro works, and Gloria Perkins, the starlet, are essential in advancing the plot—and Ettore need never have appeared on screen (indeed his part was heavily cut in filming). The others, Corrado and Giulia, Raimondo and Patrizia, the chemist and his wife, Anna's father, the old fisherman and the princeling painter, are given much more weight than their contribution to the 'action' demands. They mostly serve an altogether different purpose: to provide an environment within which the situations can develop, and which heightens the effect of the main action by making us aware of its implications or by contrasting with it.

In the opening part of the film, Claudia's stability serves to emphasize Anna's irrational, neurotic character. When Anna suddenly stops wanting to see Sandro as she arrives outside his apartment, reasonable Claudia is there saying, 'If I had a man who'd waited since midday, and I hadn't seen him for a month . . .' And during the scenes between Sandro and Anna, we see Claudia outside (first in deep focus through the bedroom window and then in intercut shots of her going towards the apartment). She wanders around, at first bored and then amused by people's reactions to an art exhibition. The normality of her behaviour contrasts with the strange silence in which Anna, having at first taken the initiative, re-

Stills: Anna and Sandro.

11

mains completely aloof while she allows Sandro to make love to her. Throughout the first part of the film, Claudia is a foil to Anna who, having nothing to occupy her but her own emotions, is completely and selfishly absorbed by them.

The use of background characters as environment is taken very much further in the scenes on the island. Giulia and Corrado, Patrizia and Raimondo are used to sketch in the *milieu* of boredom in which Anna's affair with Sandro can come to be so important to her. Boredom in Antonioni's movies is always the main component of a life devoid of any purpose except enjoyment, and reduced to a search for ways of passing the time. Patrizia has her jigsaw puzzles and her dog. Raimondo goes skin diving although he says he hates it. Corrado asks Patrizia for the flag of her yacht so that he can plant it on the island. The boredom is underlined by the presence of Claudia who is actually enjoying herself whether she is paddling among the rocks or just sitting on the yacht.

The boredom of Giulia and Corrado has another aspect with a more immediate relevance

to the Sandro/Anna situation. Giulia and Corrado are bored with each other. Their relationship has degenerated into mutual torture—the end of the road along which Sandro and Anna are moving. In their very first dialogue exchanges we are made aware of the parallel —Corrado and Giulia had come to this area twelve years before—and just look at them now:

GIULIA: The sea is as smooth as a mirror.
CORRADO: That's right, start coining clichés . . .
GIULIA: Once these islands were all volcanoes.
CORRADO: When you and I came here twelve

years ago, you were already giving geography lessons.

The first part of the film and particularly the island sequences, then, are used to fill in the necessary background to the action (here again there is rigorous exclusion of the unnecessary —for example, we never learn much about Claudia's antecedents). In the foreground,

Stills: characters in L'Avventura. *Left—Corrado (James Addams) and Sandro. Below—Patrizia (Esmeralda Ruspoli), Raimondo (Lelio Luttazzi), Giulia (Dominique Blanchar).*

Antonioni relies on our minute observation of what the characters are doing or saying. Every gesture has a precise significance and every technical device Antonioni can muster is used to help us see it. We have to observe for ourselves the build-up of the relationship between Claudia and Sandro; it is not explained to us. Socially, Claudia is an intruder from a lower class. She is given a lift to the yacht in Anna's car, and elsewhere Anna treats her in a slightly patronizing way—having her wait outside while she makes love with Sandro or offering to give her a blouse which she likes. Claudia is embarrassed by Raimondo's grotesquely half-hearted attempts to seduce Patrizia, and offers to leave them alone. She is the only one to derive any spontaneous enjoyment from the cruise: a particular gesture makes this clear—her delight when one of the yacht crew comes ashore with a bowl of fruit.

Before Anna's disappearance, there is vir-tually no contact between Claudia and Sandro. Claudia is the first to wonder where Anna is. As she says '*Anna dov'è?*' she looks at Sandro. She is the only one of the group who feels much responsibility for Anna's disappearance. Sandro's first reaction is irritation—'Anna is full of ideas.' Giulia at first enjoys the search as a new diversion, but soon she is absorbed in her own problems—'Did you see how Corrado treats me? He does everything to humiliate me.' Such selfishness shocks Claudia. Already isolated from the rest by her position —her only link with them was Anna—Claudia soon comes into conflict with them when she insists on remaining on the island. Antonioni brings out the conflict by having her walk away from the camera and from the rest of the group before she says 'I'm staying.' Then he cuts to a full-face shot of her showing determination, with the others behind her while Sandro urges her to leave. As he is staying because he feels that he should, Sandro is disturbed by Claudia's genuine feeling of responsibility. He tells her that she will be in the way—the lamest of excuses for getting rid of her. Corrado is staying to get away from Giulia—

CORRADO: I'm staying too.
GIULIA: Why? What if it rains?
CORRADO: If it rains, I'll buy an umbrella.

Throughout the subsequent scene in the fisherman's hut, the tension between Claudia and the men, particularly Sandro, is conveyed through a favourite Antonioni device—she avoids looking at them. Even the least perceptive critics noticed without help that on the whole, people didn't look at each other in *L'Avventura*. What they failed to see was the expressive use that Antonioni makes of the direction in which his characters are looking. If they look each other straight in the eye, there is an emotional reason for it; if they don't, there's

Still: Anna and Claudia.

Still: the search—Giulia, more absorbed with her own problems, and Claudia.

a reason for that too.

The conflict between Sandro and Claudia eventually becomes explicit when the old man asks what has happened:

SANDRO: Nothing . . . nothing.

Claudia turns, amazed, to look at him.

CLAUDIA: Why not tell him?

Then, to the old man—

CLAUDIA: A girl who was with us has disappeared.

The old man seems frankly surprised at this.

OLD MAN: How do you mean disappeared? . . . Drowned?

CLAUDIA: Not drowned . . . Disappeared, we don't know where she is.

SANDRO: And it's my fault. Say that as well. You're thinking it.

CLAUDIA: Rather than minding so much about my thoughts, you would have done better to try to understand what Anna was thinking.

Claudia looks at Sandro only when she is outraged enough to clash with him. When she runs out into the rain, calling for Anna, her action

15

is an expression of her feelings of responsibility for Anna. Sandro's part in the whole scene reflects his inability to appreciate spontaneously the feelings of other people.

Sandro is much less aware than Claudia or Anna of the relevance of other people to his own life—he did not realize, as Anna did, the implications for them in Corrado's relationship with Giulia. He did not notice her problems and made unwittingly crude and hurtful remarks. In his last conversation with Anna we can find the final motivation for her disappearance:

ANNA: The thought of losing you makes me want to die, but I don't feel you any more.
SANDRO: Didn't you feel me yesterday?
Corrado and Giulia pass in the background.
ANNA: Why must you ruin everything?

As he does not respond to the feelings of other people, he does not feel any responsibility for what happens to them. His emotional superficiality seems in Antonioni's eyes to be a corollary to lack of purpose in life—it is shared by everyone except Claudia, who comes from outside their social class, and Anna, because of her neurotic concentration on her own feelings.

The morning after the scene in the hut, Claudia apologizes to Sandro for her actions the previous evening (something which none of the others would do), and he asks her whether Anna ever mentioned him (a typically egocentric question). He is now wondering why Anna disappeared, but the conversation also provides his first contact with Claudia which is free from hostility. It is slight and uncertain— they avoid looking at each other except for an exchanged glance when they hear a boat passing. Their feelings about Anna remain significantly different:

Stills: Anna and Sandro—The last conversation (above) and the previous day (left).

SANDRO: She acted as if all the affection— mine, yours, her father's—meant nothing to her.

CLAUDIA: I wonder what I could have done to have avoided all this.

Sandro on the make for his fiancée's best friend is a spectacle which would, by Hayes Code morality, mark him down for summary retribution—particularly as he's doing this when his fiancée might have committed suicide.

17

But Antonioni does not condemn Sandro or invite us to do so. He has even gone so far as to say that Anna's disappearance creates a gap that is immediately filled by other factors.

Why should we condemn Sandro for his actions? It's not moral unawareness that prevents Antonioni from judging Sandro: his films could be summed up as a critique of society by way of its moral precepts. The complex of reasons underlying the refusal to condemn Sandro is central to the whole of Antonioni.

In the first place, judgment implies the acceptance of standards. But what standards? 'We make do with obsolete moral standards, out-of-date myths, old conventions,' said Antonioni at his press conference to introduce L'Avventura at Cannes, and elsewhere in the same statement he referred to 'emotional traits which . . . condition man without offering him any help, . . . tie him down without showing him a way out. And yet it seems that he has not yet managed to rid himself of this heritage.'

Antonioni frequently compares the scientific and moral progress of mankind: 'Man is prepared to rid himself of technological and scientific concepts when they turn out to be false. Never has science been so humble or ready to retract. But in the field of emotions there is total conformism. In recent years we have studied feelings to the point of exhaustion. We have been able to do that, but not to find new answers or even to get a clue to a solution of the problem.'

The rejection of 'obsolete' moral standards could mean the substitution of a personal code according to which actions are judged. But Antonioni does not propose a replacement and therefore refrains from judgments. 'I'm not a moralist,' he insists (and one can only agree on the most superficial level). 'My film is neither a denunciation nor a sermon.'

He would not, I'm sure, allow that he had the right to condemn Sandro's actions, for the implication would be that he was in some way superior to Sandro, an ideal which would hardly appeal to Antonioni who has in his film totally abandoned the 'superannuated casuistry of positives and negatives', as Tommaso Chiaretti remarks in his introduction to the published script of L'Avventura. Thus 'there are no heroes in Antonioni's films, only protagonists.' Being himself a product of the *milieu* which he depicts in his films, Antonioni does not believe that he is qualified to judge his characters. 'The middle class doesn't give me the means with which to resolve any middle class problems. That's why I confine myself to pointing out existing problems without proposing any solutions.'

Because we are not expected to identify with any of the characters or to judge them as individuals (the latter tends to be a consequence of the former), we are left free to draw more general conclusions. We are expected, for example, to see Sandro as a representative of his class and even of his society and time. It is hardly surprising that Scott Fitzgerald is one of Antonioni's favourite authors.

Sandro in pursuit of Claudia does not present at all the appearance which might be expected from a man on the make. One never feels that he is taking the initiative at all, but that he is dragged along by an impulse which he cannot control.

On the morning after Anna's disappearance, Claudia has just washed her face in a pool of rain water when Sandro comes down towards her. She glances at him, then looks away and begins to walk off up the slope. Sandro grasps her hand and she turns towards him before breaking away without a word. His look could hardly be further from aggressive male supremacy: it seems rather to say 'Please help me.' He behaves here and later more as a suppliant than as a seducer. To Sandro, insecure and fearful of what might have happened, Claudia seems to provide the possibility of support or escape. It is almost as if he needs a mother as much as a mistress: a bosom to bury his face in as an escape from the unpleasantness of the world.

In this he fits Antonioni's picture of modern man which he laid out in his 1960 Cannes statement. There he contrasted Renaissance man, filled with the joy of living and doing in an apparently Ptolemaic, earth-centred universe, and his modern counterpart, whose world is Copernican, a tiny fragment of an infinite universe. Result: man has lost his feeling of dominance and is filled with fear and uncertainty. Now this is the sort of glib explanation that should be suspect for explaining too much too simply. However, the historical explanation is not particularly important: what matters is the picture of man trapped between his own fears and moral restraints from which he cannot escape.

Back to Sandro, chasing after Claudia. He continues as pathetically as he started. The confined space of the yacht cabin brings them

Still: the yacht cabin.

so close together when he comes below deck to look for his suitcase that he manages to make up his mind to take her in his arms and kiss her. For a moment her response is definitely co-operative before she breaks away and rushes out on deck, leaving Sandro looking stunned. When they reach the Sicilian mainland, he follows her to the railway station and on the train, almost begging her all the time to let him stay. His approach is enough to make even Claudia tell him to stop looking so tragic. There is never any suggestion that his misery is the standard lovelornness gambit—it seems perfectly genuine.

Sandro's yen for Claudia derives partly from his insecurity: he needs comforting as well as the boost to his ego that would come from her seduction. He finds refuge from his troubles in his over-riding impulse—desire is only part of it—for Claudia. Antonioni sees this as a general condition: the world is sexually awry because men have found in a compulsive eroticism some diversion from their problems. 'Why do you think that eroticism has flooded into literature and entertainment? It is a symptom (perhaps the easiest one to perceive) of the emotional sickness of our time . . . man is uneasy . . . so he reacts, but he reacts badly, and is unhappy.'

Antonioni sets out to show us that the urge that has taken hold of Sandro is not something particular and therefore significant only on a personal level. Throughout the film we are presented with sexual behaviour that is silly, lewd, or grotesque. On the yacht there is Raimondo greedily caressing various items of a resigned Patrizia's anatomy. There are the young men of Messina, induced to riot as a publicity gimmick for a well-stacked starlet. She appears in a dress that is distended slightly past bursting point so that a torn seam on her thigh proffers the repressed locals a calculatedly arousing peep at her underclothes. Equally grotesque are the comic efforts of the little

gardener in the train to get into conversation with a servant girl. And when Claudia finally goes to Sandro there is the chemist at Troina whose surliness is suddenly dropped as she appears: he becomes friendly so that he can have more time to admire her legs, to the fury of his young wife. The peasants in the market place at Noto who gather round to gape at Claudia are possessed by the same sad compulsion as Sandro: sex in Antonioni's eyes has degenerated from a joyful expression of emotion into a gloomy means of escape.

When Sandro grasps Claudia's hand for the first time, her look as she gazes down at him (he is a little downhill from her) is sufficient to indicate her determination to resist and not to be distracted from the search. At their next encounter, her resolution falters. In this scene, as often with Antonioni, the leading part is taken not by either of the characters but by the setting. The embrace is provoked by their sudden proximity to each other, which in turn is a direct result of the confined space in the yacht cabin.

If it is the product of an environmental accident, the responsibility of the characters is diminished. In Antonioni's world, actions are often determined as much by the surroundings as by the people themselves—either in an immediate and physical way by the setting or by conditioning from the environment which tends to limit their choice. At times Claudia and particularly Sandro seem to be activated more by social and environmental forces than by their own decisions. Thus placed outside the area of individual moral judgments, their actions take on a wider significance. Claudia's action in kissing Sandro goes against everything she has previously felt (remember her horror at Giulia's concern with her own situation during the search). Antonioni makes his characters re-

Still: use of setting—Claudia's isolation.

tain a human unpredictability. They do not perform actions worked out to be consistent with a thesis. In fact this sort of unreasoned but not gratuitous action is of the greatest importance to Antonioni. 'I wanted to show that sentiments which convention and rhetoric have encouraged us to regard as having a kind of definite weight and absolute duration, can in fact be fragile, vulnerable, subject to change. Man deceives himself when he hasn't courage enough to allow for new dimensions in emotional matters—his loves, regrets, states of mind—just as he allows for them in the field of technology.' In this light Claudia's action in the cabin scene is not at all a matter for condemnation. She is beginning to face up to the new emotional situation of her desire for Sandro. But her spontaneous action lasts only until she has had time to realize what she is doing. Then she breaks away from Sandro and goes ashore.

Claudia is torn between her want for Sandro and her feelings of responsibility for Anna. In the scenes at the railway station where Sandro comes to find her, responsibility is winning, but only just. She can look directly and confidently at Sandro for 'I know it's difficult, but don't make things more complicated. Above all don't look so tragic.' But the confidence is stretched thinly over uncertainty and fear: 'And don't wait for the train to leave,' (looking straight and imploringly at him) 'I beg you.' This is hardly the line to succeed with self-centred Sandro, and sure enough, after only a moment's hesitation he is chasing after her train. For the first shots of Claudia in her compartment, she is looking straight at the camera in quite a close shot, indicating determination, but as the conversation proceeds, the camera retreats. The sequence is made up of intercut shots of Sandro and Claudia emphasizing the lack of communication between them. She is saying 'remember only three days ago. . . . Does it take so little to make you forget? . . . I never felt so awful

in my life. Sandro, please help me.' While she is speaking, it starts to rain. Through the carriage window, we see waves crashing on the shore by the railway line. In addition to their emotional feeling, both the rain and the sea link back to the scenes on the island.

The scene of the little gardener and the servant girl in the next compartment gives a break in the emotional tension, and the reactions of Sandro and Claudia tell us more about them. Claudia laughs freely and openly, while Sandro's amusement is a little forced, almost calculated. The incident furnishes him an opportunity to catch hold of Claudia's hand again. Her smile disappears immediately as she looks round at him. She breaks away. Again we are presented with the contrast between their approaches to life—Claudia's is basically spontaneous, although conditioned by her feelings of responsibility; Sandro's is intellectual—each step is thought out before it is taken, and his spontaneous actions are usually very clumsy.

Two sequences later, after the Gloria Perkins episode and Claudia's arrival at the villa where the rest of the yacht party are staying, we see Claudia sitting in her room waiting with excited anticipation for the arrival of Sandro. She has made her decision.

Claudia's excitement is seen in the self-consciously elegant way she selects a ring from her jewel box and puts it on. This is echoed in the elegance of the decor and the sensuous qualities of the photography—the images have suddenly gained a sort of lustre. In this first shot of the sequence, Claudia is sitting on a chair on which is draped a frilly white slip. It forms a contrasting fringe around her black dress and gives the whole image extra impact. The excitement is also carried in the music—a

Still: Sandro profits by the incident in the train to take hold of Claudia's hand.

bubbling little tune for flute and piano. The expectant feeling continues through into the extraordinary sequence in which the blonde Claudia puts on a black wig and Patrizia wears a blonde one. One notices that Patrizia assumes a new personality with her wig, whereas Claudia, who has a personality of her own, does not. Claudia's new feelings are even sufficient to carry her through the scenes between Giulia and the young prince, which would

Still: Claudia and the wig.

normally have embarrassed her (like the spectacle of Raimondo on the make for Patrizia). The image of unfaithfulness might also have troubled her because of its relevance to Sandro. This sequence also helps fill in a background of sexual availability which makes it easy for Sandro to be tempted by Gloria Perkins at the end of the film. In this *milieu*, too, the exam-

Still: Claudia with Giulia and the young artist.

ples with which Claudia is constantly presented help undermine her resolve and pave the way for her affair with Sandro.

In *L'Avventura* there are two main elements which provide the environment for the action: the sexual looseness of the secondary characters, and the barrenness and/or solitude of the locations—the island, the deserted village, the train without passengers, and the hotel on the morning after the party.

'In this film,' said Antonioni, 'the landscape is a component of primary importance. I felt the need to break up the action by inserting, in a good many sequences, shots which could seem banal or of a documentary nature (a whirlwind, the sea, dolphins, etc.). But in fact these shots are essential because they help the idea of the film: the observation of a state of

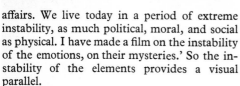

Stills: Giulia and the painter.

affairs. We live today in a period of extreme instability, as much political, moral, and social as physical. I have made a film on the instability of the emotions, on their mysteries.' So the instability of the elements provides a visual parallel.

Throughout the film, the locations and even the climatic conditions play a crucial part in its development. Anna's home, which is glimpsed in the opening sequence, and Sandro's rather precious flat help to characterize them. In addition to its function as a symbol of barrenness, the island location allows us to see the characters separated from the *milieu* in which they are accustomed to operate. In this setting we are able to see them deprived of their normal time-occupying routine. The storm which gathers as the search progresses contributes to the increasing seriousness of the situation. In one shot—Claudia on a rocky promontory with waves crashing around it—the location is used to show us the desperateness of Claudia's isolation, another factor which drives her towards Sandro.

None of the effects which Antonioni obtains would be as powerful in studio sets. 'It's true that on the set you can construct interior and exterior as you please. But for me something is missing, an occasional quality of reality,

perhaps even a particular light. In a sense, I can say that to direct in a natural setting is to continue writing the film.' He is always ready to take advantage of any opportunity which he discovers on location, and when he allows himself a *jeu d'esprit*, it usually stems directly from the location, whose reality it helps to establish. The script was modified in shooting to accommodate the old fisherman from Australia, because he really lived on the island, and Antonioni found him interesting. The idea for the Gloria Perkins riot (which as I've mentioned is more than light relief) came from a newspaper story. (Its setting, Messina, and the girl, Dorothy de Poliolo, are those of the original incident.) Antonioni has said that working on location puts him in a similar position to a painter who has to fill a certain wall with frescoes. As the painter exploits the irregularities of a wall for decorative effect, so the director takes advantage of the unexpected circumstances which occur on location to enliven his film.

Most of the time, though, the setting is used as a part of the main action. The barrenness of the countryside where Claudia and Sandro

make love for the first time echoes the scenery of the island, while the railway train which passes (apart from its slightly too obvious sexual symbolism) takes us back to the train scene when Claudia's feeling of responsibility was last strong enough to make her reject Sandro.

These feelings are now rapidly turning to shame. Claudia, waiting outside the hotel in Noto while Sandro goes in to look for Anna, becomes aware that all the men hanging

Stills: The first love scene (right); Noto.

Still: the hardware shop.

around the main square are staring at her. She rushes into a hardware shop to hide. Outside again with Sandro, she says, 'If you said, "Claudia, I love you," I'd believe you. . . . I'd make you swear to all kinds of things. . . . It wouldn't be fair. . . . When I think you said it all before to Anna. . . .' In her shame, she is still worried about whether she is being fair to Sandro. Her problem is very different from Anna's—she is worried about whether Sandro loves her, not about her feeling for him, of which she is certain.

The relevance of the background to the foreground becomes crucial in the Noto sequences. We learn from Sandro's monologue on the bell tower that he is an architect who has given up his creative ambitions for the easy money he could make by the purely mechanical job of estimating. The reawakening of these ambitions is connected with his feelings for Claudia. The first time we were aware that architecture had any particular significance for Sandro was in the first scene back on the mainland—in the police station at Milazzo. The building chosen for the sequence

was a very remarkable baroque villa. The script was modified at this point to show Sandro's interest in architecture. He is staring at part of the building with such obvious interest that someone comes up to him and points out a bust of the man for whom it was built. 'I bet he's turning in his grave'—at the use to which it has been put: a fine building turned into a police station—a token of what's happened to Sandro: architect turned into calculating machine.

In the scene on the bell tower in Noto, Sandro's feelings for Claudia come to be linked more closely to his architectural ambitions. We see Sandro against a background of buildings talking to Claudia with mounting enthusiasm:

SANDRO: Look at this imagination, this exuberance, this preoccupation with setting. What extraordinary freedom. . . .

A pause during which he continues to look in front of him. Then reflectively:

SANDRO: I really must make up my mind to leave Ettore. . . . I'd like to start working again on my own projects. You know, I've plenty of ideas. . . .

Claudia has calmed down (this comes after the guilt scene in the square outside the hotel) and is watching him with interest.

CLAUDIA: And why have you given them up?

SANDRO: One day I was asked to make an estimate for a school. I realized that I had made four million lire in 36 hours. Since then, I've gone on making estimates for other people's jobs.

Claudia looks at him as if judging him, and Sandro notices it.

SANDRO: Why are you looking at me like that?

CLAUDIA: On the contrary, I'm sure that you could produce many beautiful things.

SANDRO: I don't know. What use are beautiful things now? How long do they last?

He says this with a touch of sadness, and avoids looking at Claudia. Then he smiles to himself and is silent. He looks again for a little at the outlines of the buildings. A moment later he turns to Claudia.

SANDRO: Claudia, are we going to get married?

With the feelings which Claudia has reawakened in Sandro has come rediscovery of his vocation as an architect. It is quite natural, therefore, for him to go on from describing his ambitions and doubts as an architect to proposing to Claudia, for both are manifestations of the same emotional state. In a way, Claudia has become the personification of Sandro's vocation.

She is amazed and disturbed by Sandro's proposal, and for the time being rejects it. Her hair blows across her face just as it did in the morning scenes on the island as she says 'What can I answer? . . . No. Not yet, at least. . . . I don't know. . . . I'm not even thinking about us. How can you ask at a time like this.' Although she rejects his proposal, she is overjoyed by this evidence that he has some feeling for her. Her accidental ringing of one of the bells gives her a way of showing her joy (this too was improvised in shooting). The reflection of the sound of the bells back from the buildings which Sandro has been talking about is a symbolic comment on the whole sequence.

An even more striking expression of Claudia's joy follows. A loudspeaker van draws up in the square of Noto, scattering leaflets. From it comes *'una musichetta volgare e molto ritmata'*. We cut to the room where Claudia is rummaging behind the bed for her stockings. Putting them on becomes the beginning of an impromptu dance around Sandro who doesn't have her natural high spirits. The sordidness of the room makes the radiance of the dance even more stunning. As Sandro goes out having managed no more in the way of response than a slight quizzical smile, Claudia playfully blocks the doorway and says in a mock dramatic tone, 'You can't leave me alone in a hotel room.' She adds 'And tell me . . . that you love me,' but her last words have become genuinely serious as she has noticed Sandro's lack of response. This seriousness is strengthened by the contrast with her previous high spirits.

But Antonioni very soon makes it even plainer that nothing much has changed in Sandro. He goes to the local museum to absorb more inspiration. It is closed and there's no one who can tell him how to get in, or when it opens. This setback, in contrast to the aspirations he has rediscovered, opens the way for his fit of jealousy when he sees the young architect drawing. Here is a young man actually producing something. He knocks over the ink bottle and blots out the picture simply because he is jealous of the young man, who still has the idealism and creativeness that Sandro has lost. That's why he asks the man's age and says, 'When I was 23 I used to look harder for fights, and find them. . . .'

Still: 'You can't leave me alone in a hotel room.'

Stills: Claudia refuses to let Sandro make love to her.

When he returns peevishly to the hotel, he seems to the sensitive Claudia quite a different person from her new lover. Because of this, she refuses to let him make love to her.

SANDRO: What's wrong—

CLAUDIA: Sandro . . . wait a moment, just a moment. I feel as if I don't know you.

SANDRO: You should be delighted. It's a new adventure.

CLAUDIA: What did you say?

SANDRO: I was only joking, of course. Can't I make jokes? Now tell me why you don't want to.

CLAUDIA: Oh, Sandro . . . I want everything you do, but . . .

But she is unable to communicate with him. Sandro has treated Claudia in this sequence in almost the same way as he did Anna before she disappeared.

The last part of the film puts Sandro for the first time with Claudia on what is more or less home ground for him. She has now recovered herself—there are happy gestures and embraces behind the hotel porter. Claudia is tired and prepares for bed while Sandro dresses for the evening. He talks about his ambitions to her. 'I used to dream of being a diplomat. I never saw myself as very rich. I saw myself as a genius working in a garret. Now I've got two flats and I've neglected to become a genius.'

Downstairs Sandro is without Claudia, the image of his new aspirations. Furthermore, he is in his normal *milieu*. In the circumstances it is easy for him to be defeated. Claudia and vocation are betrayed at almost the same time. His capitulation to Ettore is a form of unfaithfulness to Claudia. He makes a half-hearted attempt to talk to Ettore. ('Let's take a walk first') but has no reply to his 'Can I count on you tomorrow. . . . Without your figures I'm sunk. . . .' Already Sandro has exchanged a meaningful glance with Gloria Perkins, whom we know from the comments of the journalist in Messina to be strictly a cash proposition. There is an extraordinary image through which Antonioni expresses his disgust for the situation, personal and social. Sandro passes behind an elegantly dressed girl looking at a painting. It shows a young woman breast-feeding an old man. The girl looks round and smiles provocatively at Sandro, revealing her ugliness. After the conversation with Ettore, we see Gloria again. So does Sandro. He goes to watch tele-

Still: arrival at the hotel; Claudia and Sandro with Patrizia.

vision, but is soon bored with it. Cut to Claudia waiting happily. She wanders into Sandro's room, does a little dance with his shirt and makes faces in a mirror before going to bed.

Claudia still waiting at dawn is not at all happy. The camera looks out of her window towards the sea. The coldness of the view is taken up by the plaintive flute music. We hear train noises in the distance, like the sea a reminder of earlier sequences. So is the black sweater which Claudia is wearing—she wore it in both the scenes where she rejected Sandro because of Anna. But Anna now seems a threat

to the new position Claudia has just managed to accept. She says to Patrizia, 'I'm afraid that Anna has come back . . . that they're together. . . . At first the idea of Anna's death almost killed me. Now I don't cry any more. I'm afraid she's alive.' Claudia is very worried indeed as she runs down corridors looking for Sandro. She finds him with Gloria Perkins on a couch in among the debris of the previous night's party. She rushes out. Gloria says 'Caro' to

Sandro and gets slapped. She asks for a 'souvenir' and Sandro throws a couple of notes down. She picks them up with her bare feet.

The final scene in the hotel car park relies on montage to show the isolation of Sandro and Claudia. Elsewhere Antonioni often used the structure of a single shot for this—many of his compositions are very dislocated. We see Claudia walking across the car park with a church tower in the background. A close shot of the back of her head with the rest of the screen filled by a weeping willow tree. Sandro coming out of the hotel. A close shot of Claudia crying, and then a long shot from behind her as Sandro comes and sits in the foreground. Then there is a series of intercut close-ups of them weeping. Claudia has come to stand behind Sandro with her hand on the back of the seat. She raises it to touch his head, hesitates and lowers it. Then she finally manages to make a gesture of forgiveness by stroking his hair. All this is shown in a series of close-ups of faces and hands. Sandro and Claudia are united again in the final long shot.

It is hardly a happy ending—the fade-out music is discordant and behind them in the last shot are an expanse of blank wall and mountains covered in snow. But it is easier to find some optimism in it than in any of Antonioni's other films except perhaps La Notte.

Claudia has lost a certain purity of purpose which made the love scenes lyrically exuberant. (In the published script there is a dialogue exchange with Patrizia on the yacht, suggesting that Claudia is a virgin.) At the end she is thrown for the first time into the sort of emotional turmoil which is a commonplace for the others. But having vastly more personality than they, she will recover. She will—as Antonioni has said—not leave Sandro. 'She will stay with him and forgive him. For she realizes that she too, in a certain sense, is somewhat like him. Because—if for no other reason—from the moment she suspects Anna may have returned, she becomes so apprehensive, so afraid she may be back and alive that she begins to lose the feeling of friendship she once had for Anna, just as he had lost his affection for Anna and perhaps is also beginning to lose it for her. But what else can she do but stay with him?' They will stay together out of 'a mutual sense of pity' —and of shame which Claudia shares as she has contributed to his downfall by abandoning him to his friends. And perhaps with the help of Claudia, Sandro will somehow find the strength to give up his comfortably lucrative job and resume his vocation.

Sandro may not be any less weak than he was previously but at least he has found some feeling of responsibility for the way his actions affect others or, at any rate, Claudia. Sandro's irresponsibility, his lapsed vocation and his unsatisfactory love affair at the beginning of the film are all bound up together and related to the weakness of his social environment. As Chiaretti says in his introduction to the script, 'L'Avventura could not have taken place except in an anaemic milieu like that of the Italian bourgeoisie.'

This, I think, is the core of the film: on a general level, the connection between the condition of a society and its morality; individually the integration of sexual behaviour with the rest of the personality—for instance, the relevance of Sandro's emotional life to his work. Sartre has expressed a similar view, talking in a newspaper interview about the necessity of building a bridge between Marx and Freud: 'Freud was the first to say something that seems to me of capital importance: that everything which makes a man has meaning. . . . What matters is his demonstration that sexual desire is not simply sexual desire, but something that will encroach on a man's whole personality, even affecting the way he plays the piano or the violin.'

SHORTS

L'Avventura was Antonioni's sixth feature. In his first five long films and the seven shorts which preceded them, he worked out the methods which he finally used with complete success in *L'Avventura*.

The rather spare visual quality of Antonioni's films is already evident in his second short, *N.U.* (1948), which was about street-cleaning in Rome. Its last shots are unmistakably Antonioni's. It is dusk and the street-cleaners are returning home. A train is heard offscreen. The last shot of the film shows the train which carries the street-cleaners (or perhaps it is their day's sweepings; I forget). It moves across the frame to reveal a wide, bare, and very clean road. In *N.U.* Antonioni rejects all the formal trappings of documentary—or at least Italian documentary—aiming as always for 'truth rather than logic' and building his film not from planned sequences but from lots of small fragments. The technique is continued in *Superstizione* (1949), a series of very short scenes making up a sort of catalogue of superstitious practices.

In *L'Amorosa Menzogna* (also 1949) the dream of the title is provided by the *fumetti*, picture magazines which tell stories in strip-cartoon form, but with photographs instead of drawings. The film opens with photographs being taken for a story, and goes on to show the lives of the 'stars' of the *fumetti*. Far from being the romantic figures of their audience's dreams, they are ordinary working people—the hero, for instance, is a garage mechanic. Already Antonioni is interested in people first as individuals, rather than as symbolic figures, or representatives of a social condition. This marks him off from the neorealists, although his first film, *Gente del Po* (shot in 1943, but not edited and shown until 1947) apparently had much in common with neorealist movies made much later. Because of his concern with individuals, Antonioni is able to reach his audience on a much more personal level than de Sica, say, in *Bicycle Thieves*, where the approach (personalization of a social situation) and the rather rudimentary level of characterization kept the audience aware that it was looking in from outside on someone else's problems. Antonioni said: 'The events and situations of the day were extraordinarily unusual, and perhaps the most interesting thing to examine at that time was the relationship between the individual and society. It really wasn't necessary to know the protagonist's inner thoughts. . . . However, when I started making films, things were somewhat different and my approach therefore was also different.' The limitation of aims inherent in the strict neorealist approach made it inadequate for Antonioni. The examination of social evils in a limited area has never been his primary aim. He works on two levels: a critique of the structure of modern society, and an investigation of individual behaviour. In showing the interconnection of each with the other, he needs to make the audience feel that the lives of the characters are relevant to their own. Perhaps it is this more sophisticated expression of a Marxist viewpoint that has floored some critics. The overtly left-wing cinema has been restricted for so long to facile and often patronizing statements of sympathy for the victimised proletariat that appreciation of the all-embracing Marxism of Antonioni requires some effort on the part of the audience.

CRONACA DI UN AMORE

The overt social content of Antonioni's early films is greater than in *L'Avventura* or *Il Grido*. His first feature, *Cronaca di un amore* (1950) centres on the social barriers between a girl of working-class background who has married money, and her lover who has remained poor. It does not have the structure of a traditional social-comment movie, but is mainly concerned with presenting an ironical picture of the results of human actions.

A rich Milanese engineer, afraid that his young wife Paola is being unfaithful, calls in a private detective. The investigator starts work in Paola's home town, and soon learns that a friend of Paola's was killed in an elevator accident some years previously. News of the

Frame: Paola (Lucia Bosè) goes to the opera.

investigation reaches Guido, Paola's former lover, from whom she parted because of their feelings of guilt at the accident, which they could have prevented. As a result, Guido moves to Milan, starts seeing Paola again, and once more becomes her lover.

When Enrico tells her about the investigations (which have not yet revealed anything) she has to reassure him by letting him make love to her. Next day she tells Guido, who naturally but unreasonably goes off in a rage. Still she cannot stay away from him for long. The situation is now intolerable for them: she needs Guido, but cannot do without the luxury to which she is accustomed. A playful suggestion from her that they might murder Enrico hardens into a serious plan. One evening Guido waits with a revolver at a bridge on Enrico's route home, where he will have to slow down. However, Enrico has read the detective's report of Paola's infidelity. Before he reaches the bridge, his car crashes into a ditch—perhaps through recklessness, but per-

Frame: Paola with Guido (Massimo Girotti) in his room.

haps it is suicide. Either way, the responsibility lies with Paola and Guido. Hearing the car explode, Guido cycles to the scene of the crash. After he has seen the body, he hastens home and packs his bags. Paola panics when the police arrive. She escapes through the back door and drives to Guido's lodgings, in time to catch him as he is leaving. He tells her that Enrico has killed himself. When she has recovered sufficiently from the shock to realize that Guido is leaving, she implores him to telephone her the next day. He says that he will, and gets into the taxi that is waiting for him, telling the driver to take him to the station.

Cronaca and *La Signora senza camelie* are much darker in feeling than *L'Avventura*—actions never have the hoped-for result, because of people's inability to realize how others—or even they themselves—will react. In every interview he gives, Antonioni talks about the fragility of emotions. The characters in the early films are totally unable to allow for emotional changes, and so all actions calculated to produce a particular result are doomed to failure. It was not until *L'Avventura* that Antonioni could see any way out of the gloom.

The sensitivity to objects and locations that distinguished *L'Avventura* is already to be found in *Cronaca*. Antonioni has said, 'I have a great feeling for things, perhaps more than for people, although the latter interest me more.' He is able to use his feeling for things to aid him in describing the action which is psychological rather than physical, internal rather than external. It is often not obvious from what the characters are doing, but must be suggested through the way they are shown. Antonioni had realized that the human face is a rather inexpressive object when isolated from its surroundings in a close-up. He used no big close-ups at all. Instead he paid particular attention to the relationship of the characters with their setting. The insolubility of Paola's problem in *Cronaca* is demonstrated through her unease in Guido's room, which, by the meanness of its furnishings, represents his social class and the level of poverty to which she would have to descend if she went away with him. This unease contrasts with their happiness at just being together again when they first meet after his arrival in Milan. They are untroubled by class barriers, because the bare neutral countryside does not typify any particular social status.

Apart from the simple social contrast of Paola in Guido's room, there are more sophisticated uses of environment. As Enrico drives to his death, we see shots of Paola waiting nervously at home, photographed with highkey elegance—an angle shot includes a chandelier in the foreground of the picture. Meanwhile Guido, out in the cold, on the bridge, wanders nervously up and down in the darkness. Again the point is a social one, but elsewhere backgrounds are used for atmosphere or symbolic effect. The lovers' second meeting begins in a planetarium. The scene is shot so that the projector is in dark silhouette behind them, a grotesque shape that seems to represent the threat to their relationship. And on the bridge as they plan Enrico's murder, they are seen from a slightly high angle to include a background of men raking out muck from the drained canal below.

In *Cronaca* much more than in the later films, Antonioni relies on significant objects as well as environments. The props, too, are sometimes used to emphasize social distinctions—Paola's white fur bedspread, and Guido's cheap Nazionali cigarettes, one of the most important images of the world Paola cannot return to. More often the significant props are used as symbols: the string of pearls which Paola knocks off the bedside table and on to the floor during her first conversation (on the telephone) with Guido; a pair of huge vermouth

bottles, thirty or forty feet high, on either side of the quiet country road on which Enrico is testing the Maserati—a symbol of the inherent disorientation of a capitalist society; Paola's silk evening dress which trails on the muddy streets as she rushes to find Guido after Enrico's death.

There is one key scene in *Cronaca* which unites all the elements in the film. It comes after Paola has learned of the investigation. She is talking to Guido on a staircase around (significantly) an elevator shaft. As she says that she had to make love to her husband, a messenger boy carrying a bunch of flowers passes. (Enrico had sent her the key of the new

car in a bunch of flowers.) Paola's sorry tale is rounded off with the words, 'I hate him,' and under them we hear the sound of the elevator moving. A shot down the shaft shows the elevator ascending. The camera tilts up with its back to Paola and Guido as she asks him to kiss her, in a moment of typically Antonioni emotional miscalculation. Guido walks away leaving her leaning weakly against the wall of the staircase with the shadow of the bannister forming a contorted pattern across the picture. By his treatment of this simple dialogue scene, Antonioni has brought out its implications and linked it to the rest of the film.

LA SIGNORA SENZA CAMELIE

In *La Signora senza camelie* Antonioni is firing at much the same targets as in *Cronaca*. The heroine is again a socially displaced person, this time a shop girl who becomes a film star, and again she's played by Lucia Bosè. Although Bosè was perfect as Paola, she just will not pass muster as a shopgirl unable to cope with high society. If ever an actress has looked sophisticated it's Bosè. The audience finds itself in the same incredulity as the onlooker in a scene where she's rehearsing in a sword-and-bosom melo, the man who gasps, '*She's* meant to be a Calabrian peasant?' Apparently the part was intended for Lollobrigida who, at the time, would have fitted it well.

In *Signora*, and increasingly in the later films, there is little plot which can be summarized to give an idea of the film, but just a series of incidents. Before the film opens, the girl, Clara Manni, has been uprooted from her normal surroundings and thrust into the film world. Under the titles she is seen pacing up and down the deserted pavement outside the neighbourhood cinema where her first movie is being previewed. She enters the cinema and walks across to her colleagues. The camera tracks beside her, holding her lonely figure in the foreground while behind are the dark shapes of the audience, and on screen Clara the glamorous Cinecittà starlet singing a romantic song, the girl who is starting out on a promising career.

Next day, on the set of the period movie, we are introduced to Clara's new world. The director is saying 'I don't want to do the picture this way, but frankly I need the money.' To make the love scene they are shooting a bit

Still: the scene on the staircase in Cronaca di un amore.

hornier for the audience, Clara's bodice is opened. Gianni the producer who 'discovered' Clara and high-pressured her into films, cautions them, 'For goodness' sake remember the censor!' Before she has even finished the picture, Gianni is asking her to marry him. He demands an immediate answer on marriage as he did on her career in the cinema. When she hesitates, he produces her parents all a-flutter with excitement.

Gianni interrupts the picture to whip her off on a brisk honeymoon. They return in a shower of publicity to do the location scenes of the picture, but now he decides that it is not good enough for his wife. He refuses to let her finish it. Left with nothing to do she unloads her troubles on the director of the unfinished film, Ercole, known affectionately as Ercolino:

CLARA: What can I do all day? I like to buy things for the house, because I know about materials.

ERCOLINO: Would you like your parents to come?

CLARA: For heaven's sake. Then there'd be three of us bored. I'm used to working all day. When Ercolino tries to discuss with Gianni a script that Clara has read and liked, he is ranted at for his pains. Gianni is a ludicrously jealous husband. Seeing Clara give Ercolino a friendly peck on the cheek when he comes in, he makes loud kissing noises to show his disapproval. Then he lets fly at poor Ercolino. 'You want my wife to play a prostitute! I want her to appear in good films that sell abroad.' He is planning to have Clara play Joan of Arc. As far as Ercolino is concerned, the only formula is sex, religion, and politics combined—'perhaps you *could* do that with Joan of Arc'. But not

Gianni: 'I want to make Clara into a great actress. Clara, do you want to make decent films, or to appear in pornography?'

Joan of Arc is shown at the Venice Festival. Clara and Gianni take their seats at the première amid polite applause. But soon Gianni sneaks out 'to the projection box' or rather to the bar. There he is faced behind the counter with a row of photographs which mirror his ambitions for Clara. Among the pictures we recognize Katherine Hepburn, Anna Magnani, Bette Davis—and Lionel Barrymore. In the auditorium, the audience is beginning to make ribald comments. Clara, left alone, cannot stand it and leaves. So does a smooth young man in the row behind. He is Nardo, a diplomat, whom we have already seen in the villa where Clara's sword-and-bosom movie came to its sudden halt. His attempts to console the sobbing Clara as they cross the lagoon back to Venice are not motivated by sympathy but by the hope that he will be allowed to offer other consolations later on. However, when she has recovered herself, Clara goes back to her hotel without Nardo.

The setback at Venice has given her strength to put her own case to Gianni for the first time. The scene takes place in the train back to Rome. Antonioni has a particular fondness for trains— key sequences in *Le Amiche* and *L'Avventura* are also set in railway carriages.

Antonioni handles Clara's big speech in a characteristic manner. We first see her sitting in the background of the shot. Then as she starts coming out with her own views, she gets up and moves into the foreground.

Troubles begin to pile up for Gianni. In the Rome cinema where Joan of Arc has opened, he learns that it is to be taken off, and immediately after he's confronted by one of his backers who wants 60 million lire the next morning. Needing someone to talk to, Clara gets Nardo

Still: screen image—Clara (Lucia Bosè) sings.

to drive her out to a deserted spot on the Cinecittà back lot—more landscape symbolism, this time for the barrenness of Clara's life and of her work. Again she rejects Nardo. This time he's prepared to give up. We see him cancelling an order for flowers. But when he arrives home, there is Clara on the staircase. All she says is, 'Don't ask me any questions.'

She gets home late at night to find that Gianni has attempted to commit suicide because of his financial troubles. They have both given up at the same time. Gianni's condition is not serious, but when Nardo phones as the doctor is leaving with the ever-attentive Ercolino, she hangs up on him.

The next sequence is at Cinecittà. An extra gossips that 'Things haven't been going at all well between her and her husband for about a month now.' Nardo turns up on the set. Clara goes off to a deserted exterior to talk to him.

CLARA: We're trying to put things right by finishing a film which my husband didn't want me to complete. What am I to do?

NARDO: Do what you feel like.

CLARA: I must pay this debt. My marriage has become a commercial undertaking. I have to pay up.

Here we have the same irony as in *Cronaca*, and the Antonioni attitude on responsibility to other people, which on the whole is felt only by the poor or those who have been—Guido, Clara, Clelia in *Le Amiche*, and Claudia in *L'Avventura*. Nardo has no such feelings, as he demonstrates amply later.

Clara doesn't turn up at the opening of the new film. We see her mother in the cinema foyer standing in front of a huge picture of Clara, captioned with the film's title, *La Donna senza destino—Woman without a Destiny*. When her mother tells her over the phone that the film was a great success, Clara still refuses to speak to Gianni but says that she will write.

While Gianni is away on a business trip, she

goes off with Nardo. Getting into his car, she tells him that she has left a note for Gianni, saying that she is leaving him for Nardo. This is not at all what Nardo had in mind: he tells her to be careful and take back her note. 'Let's go away for a little. We'd be back by the time your husband comes home.' Clara goes indoors, picks up the letter, thinks, puts it back again, and goes out.

In a hotel with Nardo, Clara receives a phone call from Gianni, who quickly realizes that she has a man in her room. Nardo's reactions prove even to Clara, who is genuinely and naively in love with him, just what a louse he is. His first thoughts are for his career. She says bitterly. 'You'd better leave. I don't want to compromise you.' He goes out with a hasty '*Arrivederci Clara.*' She replies, more permanently, 'Addio'

Once more she needs someone to talk to. She picks her middle-aged co-star from *La Donna senza destino*, who advises her to work at her acting. 'Success has come too quickly. You've learned nothing.' When Ercolino comes to visit her, she is almost a recluse in her small hotel room surrounded by reproductions of Great Paintings, meaning, of course, Van Gogh. He tells her that Gianni is starting a new film, and persuades her to ask him for the main part. He even drives her back to the muddy desolation of Cinecittà in winter. They pass through crowds of extras dressed in costumes of various periods. When they find Gianni, he tells her that he needs a famous actress, preferably an American, and adds as a cruel consolation. 'You've still got a name that's fine—in certain sorts of part. And youth isn't eternal is it?' The desolation of the surroundings now echoes her feelings. She goes back to Ercolino and tells him that she'll take a part which she has been offered in a period movie. 'I'll never be a real actress. I realized that a few moments ago listening to Gianni.'

The producer of the film is overjoyed. He

leads her on to a tatty little set containing some Bedouin tents where a few plump girls idle around in harem kit. 'Ecco suo film,' he says with a sweep of his arm over his domain. Clara stands unhappily on the set in her luxurious fur coat, symbol of her star status. The producer rushes her over to the canteen to meet Gianni, to whom she's still under contract, collecting a brace of photographers on the way. Gianni willingly agrees to waive her contract. Now realizing that the only future left to her is in crummy movies, she gives in to the situation by telephoning Nardo and agreeing to see him again. Her complete despair is shown in her submission to Nardo on his own terms, although she knows he's selfish and worthless. In the background of the shot is Gianni, the cause of all that has happened to Clara. She puts down the telephone and joins her producer for publicity photographs. The last shot shows her managing to smile for the cameras.

La Signora senza camelie is complementary to *Cronaca* in form/content (two words for the same thing in different guises—there should be a word to cover both: form-content like mass-energy). *Cronaca* was almost an exposition of the Antonioni view of class barriers. Paola and Guido were separated because Paola had crossed the barrier into a higher class and could not return, while Guido was finally unable to cross. *Signora* builds on the essentials that have been demonstrated in *Cronaca* to show the disastrous effects of the *status quo* on one character, Clara, who, having irrevocably left her original *milieu*, finds that she is unfitted for survival in the class to which she aspires. Through their form, both plot and treatment, the two films are founded on Antonioni's concern with the structure of society. They illustrate a critique of the class system rather than superficially attacking the resulting evils.

Still: Clara in a deserted part of Cinecittà.

43

I VINTI

L'*Avventura*, La *Notte* and L'*Eclisse* are as closely linked as *Cronaca* and *Signora*, with *Le Amiche* as a bridge between the styles of the early films and the trilogy. But there are two Antonioni films which stand apart from the main course of Antonioni's development. One is *I Vinti* which was made in 1952, before *Signora*. The other is *Tentato Suicidio* (1953), Antonioni's contribution to the Zavattini-inspired episode film *L'Amore in città*. Apparently it told a true story about an attempted suicide and was acted by people who had been involved in the original incident. Antonioni has said that it belongs wholly to the neorealist movement, but that it was not the film he intended as he had been forced to mutilate it for reasons of length.

I Vinti, The Vanquished, is also an episode film, but of a very strange sort. Its title refers to the unbalanced youth of postwar Europe. The three episodes set in different countries—France, Italy, and England—are all concerned with violent death. They are introduced, at least in the British version—which has the hilariously unexpected title, *Youth and Perversion*—by a montage of newspaper cuttings and a pulp sociological commentary. Each of the episodes was filmed on location in the relevant country, using local actors speaking their own language. The intention was to show it in each of the three countries with the foreign-language episodes subtitled. Unfortunately it was never shown in Britain, was banned in France, and was only shown in a dubbed version in Italy after some censor trouble. Each episode has acquired some national style on top of Antonioni's own. Apart from a few sequences like the tram ride in the French version and the scenes on Banstead Downs in the British, it is not distinctively Antonionian.

The French episode is perhaps the best of the three. A French teenager of bourgeois background impresses his friends by flaunting wads of banknotes and signed pictures of pretty girls. The friends are sufficiently impressed to plan his death in order to get the money. They lure him out into the country on the pretext of a picnic, and one of them murders him, only to find the notes are stage money that the timid youth has used to make his extrovert friends respect him.

The Italian episode is the least interesting. It was made from a script dreamed up in a hurry after the State had refused the producer the financial aid he needed. The official objection was to the story which would form the Italian section of the film. *One of Our Sons*, as the rejected script is called, has however been published.

It is the story of a university student, Arturo Botta, who belongs to a postwar fascist group, and of his girl friend Mimma, who comes from a left-wing family—her father owns a seedy swimming pool, a pontoon floating on the Tiber. She finds out about Arturo's activities when she has to hide him at her father's swimming pool after a bomb incident. And so she is drawn into the organization to provide an alibi for Arturo. An expedition to collect plastic explosive is disguised as a picnic, and passes off well, except for some moments of panic when their car is followed, and a telling-off for Mimma who arrives home late. The plastic is made into five bombs, one of which Arturo has to test. Another picnic. As they ride out into the country on a Lambretta, Arturo talks about the imprisoned German leader of the organization. Mimma is not particularly interested, being more occupied by the prospect of making love and by worry that Arturo will catch cold: he wears summer clothes, even though it is cold, to keep up an impression of toughness. They stop on a deserted lane. Arturo brushes aside Mimma's embraces and opens his brief-case to reveal the bomb.

On the big day, the largest bomb, which was expected to produce a massacre, does not go off; the other three do little damage. Except for Arturo and Antonio, the leader of the operation, all the conspirators are arrested. Even this is hardly noticed by the newspapers: the group has failed completely. Arturo tries to get in touch with Antonio. Instead he meets a higher official who tells him that the Party needs level-headed men, not fanatics, and that he and his friends have been expelled. Arturo cannot comprehend why he, who wanted to be one of the Party's most dedicated heroes, should be thrown out. The Party, he decides, is becoming bourgeois and falling under the spell of democracy.

Still: the French episode of I Vinti. *Etchika Choureau helps Jean-Pierre Mocky on to the bus which takes them to the country and his murder.*

Stills: the Italian and British episodes. Above: a recurrent motif in Antonioni, the building site, with Franco Interlenghi. Right—at Epsom, Patrick Barr pays Peter Reynolds for his story.

Deciding that he must make the supreme sacrifice, he phones Mimma. Frightened by his talk of the sacredness of death for men in their prime, she rushes out to search for him.

He is by the swimming pontoon on the Tiber. Moored to it is a rowing boat which he launches after carefully making enough footprints for a group of people on the sandy shore. When the boat is in midstream, he takes a small tricolor flag out of his pocket and gags

himself with it. A long look around satisfies him that no one will see him from the river banks. He lies down in the boat and produces from his pocket a revolver, which he holds behind his neck so that it will look as if he has

been shot in the back. His pretended murder will draw attention to all the other martyrs of the cause, who are rotting in prison; it will spur the inactive to fight by giving them a martyr to avenge. As the other side is too weak to do the job, it must be done for them. Arturo has found the right position. His hand is steady as he aims the gun at the nape of his neck. No one hears the shot, and the boat drifts away on the current. A few hours later, the bank is crowded with police, journalists, and photographers. Everyone is wondering who will carry out the investigation. From the road above, Mimma looks on tearfully.

The story finally used for the Italian episode is uninteresting, and compared to the abandoned project, even at the script stage, inadequately worked out. For the benefit of the authorities, the suggestions that political subversion occurred in Italy have been removed. Now the hero, a young Italian from a rich bourgeois family, takes part in cigarette smuggling, apparently just for kicks. One night his gang is surprised by the police. There is a fight. He is injured but escapes. His wealthy girl friend tries to help him with her car, but eventually he meets his death almost by accident. In a moment of panic while the car is being filled at a country gas station, he runs out into the road and is knocked down by a police car.

The British episode is most peculiar—at least to a native. The dialogue does not seem to have been vetted by an Englishman. In the opening scene, reporter Patrick Barr enters his office with a cheerful 'Bitterly hot today!' And the music (by Antonioni's regular composer Giovanni Fusco) is largely constructed from the Londonderry Air. The story is the only one of the three that is about perversion as well as youth. Unlike the other two heroes, the British one, Peter Reynolds, is poor. He lives in a down-at-heel South London suburb, and writes poetry

in his spare time. Barr's newspaper receives a telephone call from Reynolds reporting a murder and offering an exclusive story on the discovery of the corpse. He wants a public showcase for himself and his writing. At the inquest a verdict is returned of murder by person or persons unknown. The hero boasts of having committed the perfect murder as there is nothing to connect him with the victim. No one believes his story, so he offers the paper another story telling how he did the murder. In flashback (the only one Antonioni has ever used) we see him pick up a coarse old doll (Fay Compton) outside a cinema, take her up on to Banstead Downs and strangle her on a golf course by a railway cutting. Because of his story he is charged with murder. In court he proudly tells how he did it. He is condemned to death.

Antonioni seems much less happy outside his usual surroundings. He is equally ill at ease among the Po Valley peasants of *Il Grido*. None of the stories in *I Vinti* is dealt with at the length which Antonioni's approach requires. Only in the French one is there any real feeling in the treatment—although the flatness of handling is very apt in the British episode. The film was presumably intended to have an overall structure which would give it meaning above that of the three individual stories. Obviously the pointless and violent deaths are tokens of a troubled world. But this time, Antonioni has failed to link the specific occurrences to the general argument which, on a single viewing, seems sociologically pretty phony. The main question the film provokes one to ask is why on earth he made it. Richard Roud has suggested that it was 'an attempt to satisfy that side of him which is genuinely concerned with immediate social issues'. This may well be true, but equally it could be that, like most young artists, he wanted his second major work to be as unlike his first as possible, to avoid the impression that he could do only one thing.

LE AMICHE

At least in this period, it did seem that Antonioni could do only one thing or at least make convincing films only about one section of society. The return to home ground in *Signora* produced happier results. His next feature, *Le Amiche* (1955) was even better, and the equal of *L'Avventura*, the best of his black and white films. Unlike any of his other films, it is a literary adaptation, from Cesare Pavese's *Tra donne sole*. 'What I liked in *Tra donne sole*,' Antonioni has said in interviews, 'were the female characters and their way of living out what goes on in their inner selves. Also one of these characters is remarkably like someone I knew only too well in reality, and I wanted to talk about her, to show her . . . I was never particularly troubled by considerations of remaining faithful to Pavese's novel.'

The heroine of *Le Amiche* is yet another outsider in the world of luxury. She is Clelia, who left a poor part of Turin to work in a fashion house in Rome. Now risen to an important position in her firm, she returns to Turin at the beginning of the film to open a new fashion salon. She becomes involved with the rich of Turin when the girl who has the adjoining room in her hotel attempts to commit suicide. Rosetta is one of a group of rich young people who habitually go around together. The moving spirit of the group, Momina, is about the least likeable character in any Antonioni film—she has the heartlessness of Nardo in *La Signora* and the superficiality of Giulia in *L'Avventura* without the stupidity which mitigates Giulia's unpleasantness. Momina's appearance at the hotel is not motivated by any feeling of compassion for Rosetta, whom she dismisses as '*una cretina*'; she wants to do a little detective work to pass the time. 'Haven't you found a

letter?' she asks. 'It's customary to leave farewell letters.'

Clelia visits her premises to find that decorating work is behind schedule and the architect in charge is nowhere to be found. She is being unpleasant to his assistant when he appears, looks her up and down and says, 'You're younger than I thought.' Cesare Pedroni is another of Momina's friends. He is not at all disturbed by Clelia's anger; he tells her that jobs always look as if it will take a miracle to finish them in time, but they always get finished, 'at least in Italy. We're specialists in miracles.' As she rants, he plays a carefree little game with a light bulb. 'We'll hire some extra workers,' says Clelia. 'Naturally,' Pedroni answers, 'these people are so charming.'

Meanwhile Momina has tried to visit Rosetta who is now in hospital and discovered that she made a phone call just before she started eating sleeping tablets. At the hospital she is not allowed to see Rosetta. Only Rosetta's mother can see her, and all she can say is 'How *do* I look after a night like that?'

The next stage in Momina's detective game is to find out whom Rosetta was trying to phone. She persuades Clelia to bribe the hotel telephone operator and obtain the number. It turns out to belong to Lorenzo, another of Momina's group, and a painter.

Clelia is now beginning to feel at home among these people—'as if we were old friends. I've always been working and have never had much time to make friends, so it seems natural that we should confide in each other.' She is also attracted to Pedroni's assistant Carlo ('*un semplice*', Pedroni calls him) who lives in the working-class district where she was born. We're shown very quickly that she is going to have

the same trouble as Paola in *Cronaca*.

Momina invites Clelia to go on a picnic with her friends. Even Rosetta, now recovered, is persuaded to go by Momina who swears that no one knows about the suicide attempt. They drive out to the coast. The bareness of the beach and the dunes behind, the overcast sky and the cold wind whipping up the sea provide a background commentary on the action, and underline everyone's complete lack of enjoyment from this diversion. The sequence also serves a similar purpose to the search on the island in *L'Avventura*, which to some extent it

Still: Clelia (Eleanora Rossi Drago) begins to feel at home with her new friends, Nene (Valentina Cortese) and Momina (Yvonne Furneaux).

foreshadows—that of showing the characters detached from the surroundings on which they normally rely for their amusement. The beach scene is much denser and involves more characters at once than the search. It is the most ambitious piece of ensemble work in any Antonioni film, and perhaps the most remarkable thing he has ever done. It starts with the five girl-friends standing on a platform high above the dunes. On an impulse, Mariella, the youngest and silliest of the group, calls to the others 'Come to the sea.' And off they rush, followed by their men, across the dunes and down to their beach. But when they get there, they don't find anything to do, and wander around bored. Sometimes one or two gather and exchange a few words before they drift off. The camera takes part in this, panning and tracking around the beach, picking up a person or two, then losing them. All the time, people are moving in and out of the frame to produce untidy, aimless-looking compositions. The photography is exceedingly flat, cutting out bright highlights and deep shadows to emphasize the greyness of the occasion.

They disturb a couple necking on the beach. Momina comments to Nene:

MOMINA: I don't think a man feels anything for a woman he kisses in public.

Clelia has come up to them in time to catch Momina's comment. In extreme long shot, Cesare, Vincenzo (Mariella's brother) and Lorenzo are talking. They turn and walk out of frame—towards Rosetta.

CLELIA: Do you think so?

MOMINA: Why? Don't you mind being kissed in public?

CLELIA: Perhaps not.

Nene walks round behind Clelia and offscreen right after Lorenzo.

MOMINA: Because you like being kissed.

After producing this typical sample of her small talk, Momina hears voices coming from behind a beach hut. The camera stays with her, losing Clelia, as she goes over to have a look—always trying to find some diversion. She surprises Mariella in a clinch with Franco, boyfriend *du jour*. 'Look' she cries, 'another one.' (Another couple.) 'Well, we'll have to follow their example.' She has walked back to Clelia, the camera panning with her to include Vincenzo and Cesare in the distance. Antonioni

cuts as Momina calls after Nene, whom we see in the next shot pursuing Lorenzo on to the beach. This is by no means the longest or most complex take in the sequence. The whole thing is worked out with such consistency that it is possible to tell where each one of the nine characters is at almost any time in the sequence. Even the most detailed study on the Moviola reveals no mistakes, and no manipulation of time in the cutting. Even now that he has given up the one shot per scene technique which he used in *Cronaca*, Antonioni's scenes still have the duration that they would have in life.

Nene is pursuing Lorenzo because she fears rightly that he is after Rosetta, who in the early part of the sequence is kept in view in the background. Her presence on screen reminds us that she is a drag to the party. Occasionally she's called to or referred to uncomfortably. Mariella says to Momina 'How can you leave her so alone?' Rosetta has walked right down to the water's edge, and has to run back to avoid a wave. (The linking of Rosetta and water is to appear twice again in the film.) She walks back up the beach in time to catch the end of this exchange:

MOMINA: Nene's running to her Renzo!

MARIELLA: How boring!

(Lorenzo is of course Nene's husband.)

MOMINA: All right, Clelia takes your brother, you the blond one, Nene Lorenzo, I'll take Cesare, and Rosetta?

MARIELLA: She can kill herself, but properly —there's no one left for her.

For this the camera is looking down the beach so that in the background we see Nene walking towards Lorenzo, and Rosetta coming towards the group. She half hears Mariella's last words. A cut to the reverse direction—from behind Rosetta—shows the reactions of the group as Rosetta speaks:

ROSETTA: Well?

MARIELLA: Nothing we were just talking.

MOMINA: Mariella always talks nonsense.

MARIELLA (*annoyed*): You think you're a genius among idiots.

MOMINA: Perhaps I am.

NENE (*who has joined the group*): Are you serious?

MARIELLA: Yes, I said Rosetta . . .

MOMINA (*interrupting*): You're a fool.

The arrangement of the shot in two planes, Rosetta in the foreground and the others in the background, the closeness of their grouping, and the way in which Nene comes into the frame and joins the group, all serve to show Rosetta's isolation from the others. Mariella's behaviour is that of a girl who has nothing to interest her but herself. She can be provoked by a slight insult to become so annoyed that she acts callously, without any consideration for Rosetta.

Now Antonioni cuts to a panning shot of the three men, Cesare, Lorenzo, and Vincenzo, as they walk up to join the group. The sharp cut interrupts the flow of the sequence just as the men interrupt the conversation.

CESARE: Who's mediating?

LORENZO: What's happening?

MARIELLA: There's one girl too many and she . . .

MOMINA: I?

MARIELLA: She . . .

Momina slaps her face. The nearest men pull the two girls apart.

The next shot shows us Clelia and Rosetta standing slightly apart from the others. Clelia is not looking at all happy at what's going on, and she's the only one who genuinely wants to help Rosetta. The camera moves diagonally back to take in the rest of the group as Rosetta, who has had more than she can take, begins to speak. She walks slowly, straight through the centre of the group, pausing once or twice. The camera moves when she does, but along the outside of the group.

ROSETTA: Mariella isn't a hypocrite like you. I heard what you were saying. You're playing a ridiculous comedy. Leave me alone! I'm looking for nobody, and I won't listen to anyone, least of all to you!

Rosetta has now emerged from the group. The camera has moved back with her so that she is in the foreground as she turns to make the last remark to Momina.

MOMINA: I'm not asking you to.

CLELIA: Please stop it!

MOMINA: Patience has its limits. I'm doing everything so that the little fool won't notice how ridiculous she's made herself.

Rosetta turns away from the group, towards the camera, and sobs. The camera moves back with her as she walks on, away from the group. Lorenzo breaks away from the others to come up to her and take her arm.

LORENZO: Come, don't cry. Today's Sunday and on Sunday people are silly.

They overtake the camera which pans with them as they walk away along the beach. Rosetta turns, breaks away from Lorenzo and runs up the beach. The camera pans back with her to the group.

NENE (*to Momina*): You're driving her to despair.

MOMINA: Shut up!

Clelia runs off up the beach after Rosetta.

Again the staging of the action sums up the whole situation—Rosetta is outside the group. Then in a moment of desperation she cuts right through it, as she does metaphorically at the end of the film. Clelia and Lorenzo separate themselves from the group, as they do elsewhere, because of Rosetta. The movements are convincing as action—they seem right on the level of external behaviour as well as in their context of demonstrating feelings. By going round the outside of the group, the camera emphasizes her passage through it—which would not have been nearly as noticeable if the camera had done the obvious thing and tracked in front of her. The whole scene is remarkable for the way Antonioni always manages to have the character whose behaviour is most significant at any moment occupying the attention of the audience, without a large amount of cutting, without losing the reactions of the other characters which form the essential context by using close-ups, and above all without making the actors move falsely or unspontaneously to suit the demands of the composition.

With Rosetta out of the way, everyone starts wandering around again. Cesare and Mariella go off behind a dune, only to be disturbed by Momina who wants Cesare for herself. They are back in the routine of idle chatter and aimless philandering as if nothing had ever disturbed them. Only Nene is worried, as she fears that Rosetta will take Lorenzo from her.

Still: on the beach, Cesare (Franco Fabrizi) and Mariella (Annamaria Pancani).

In the train back to Turin, Rosetta voices her pessimism to Clelia. 'What have I to live for? To say what kind of dress I'm going to wear? And what then?' Clelia realizes what's wrong with Rosetta. She has never had time herself for boredom or emotional crises because she has had to work. Later work will provide an escape for her from personal problems. Meanwhile she prescribes it as the cure for Rosetta. Again we have a key scene set in a train, symbol of transition. As in *L'Avventura*, the main element of the scene—Rosetta's desperation, Claudia's resistance to Sandro—is very soon reversed. And the whole section of the film including the beach scene is both a physical and emotional journey for Clelia, who has begun to discover what her new friends are like.

The rest of the film is devoted to three counterpointing stories which represent three aspects of the sexual/social continuum—the central story is now of the Rosetta-Lorenzo-Nene triangle, contrasting with Clelia and Carlo, Cesare and Momina.

Nene is woken up one morning by a porter bringing Lorenzo's paintings back from the gallery. She telephones and learns that she has been asked to exhibit in a big New York gallery. Lorenzo has not. This has already been foreshadowed in the art gallery sequence when a customer asked about the ceramics which were not in the catalogue. Nene is worried that her success will break up her marriage, so all she says is 'I'll have to ask Lorenzo.'

But he is out meeting Rosetta who is in better spirits again. The photography is bright and lustrous and the location is a happy one—on high ground looking down a wooded slope to a deep valley and a river. The scene opens on a group of riders on horseback. The camera pans with them to Rosetta and Lorenzo as he asks her why she phoned him. 'I wanted to ask you to destroy my picture. I wanted there to be nothing left to remember me by.' The feelings of worthlessness had completely taken possession of her, and suicide alone was not enough.

Lorenzo, whose ego needs boosting even though he doesn't yet know about Nene's success, is flattered at the thought that he might have been the cause of Rosetta's desperation. She is already happy at being the centre of his attention. 'If I played with you, I might make you the purpose of my life, even the object of my love.' But why didn't she tell him before? 'You didn't notice and I couldn't tell you. You were going to get married.' As she admits this to him, she is backing away from him towards the river (this has a significance which becomes apparent later). To underline the linking of her with water and the idea of him driving her towards the river, the white horses, which passed them at the start of the scene, reappear down by the river as he goes forward to take her in his arms.

The contrast between this scene and the one which follows it is the contrast between *L'Avventura* and *Cronaca*, for Rosetta and Lorenzo, rich unstable girl and creative artist whose vocation has not borne fruit, are like Anna and Sandro, just as Clelia and Carlo are like Paola and Guido. Carlo takes Clelia to see some furniture for the salon. 'The shop is tiny, but the furniture is beautiful and cheap.' Cesare has already said, 'It won't do. I know that without even seeing it.' But Clelia still goes. On the way she tries to explain to Carlo what she feels for him, that in her business life she has made few personal contacts, that now she needs someone to be close to her: 'I need a little warmth.' Some of this explanation is conducted in front of a shop window filled with wedding bouquets. Carlo is rather offended by the thought that she is using him. Things get worse when she sees the furniture shop and tells him, 'There's no use going upstairs. It's not what I'm looking for.' Carlo wrongly decides that she thinks his taste just isn't good

enough for her.

She takes him to see the tenement building where she was born. 'If I hadn't moved away, we might have met here. I would probably have fallen in love with you.' (There's another journey back to somewhere from the past in *La Notte*.) Clelia, going back to her birthplace to show Carlo that she doesn't think she's better than he, now looks out of place—smartly dressed against a background of squalor.

The third story, Momina and Cesare, proceeds smoothly according to the accepted rules. She has invited him to visit her. As a cover, she has also asked all her girl-friends to tea. This tea party, which goes on until Cesare arrives and the girls all dutifully file out, is almost as stunning as the beach scene in its handling. It is dominated by Momina, both directly and through the setting, her apartment, which determines the shape of the scene.

Clelia is the last of the girls to arrive. She tells Momina that Rosetta hasn't shown up at the salon. 'She won't come,' says Momina. 'Does she expect me to beg her forgiveness on my knees?' Through their reaction to Rosetta's nonappearance we come to understand a little more about the girls.

MARIELLA: Pity! Now we can't go out together any more.

CLELIA: I could use her now.

MOMINA: Why should she work?

CLELIA: To take her mind off things.

MOMINA: There are better ways.

Clelia is still upset by Carlo's inability to cope with her attitude to him, something which she had unthinkingly not expected. She decides to call the salon to see if Rosetta is there, but Nene says she will do it. Momina is prompted to offer a little advice in the light of her

Still: Rosetta (Madeleine Fischer) arrives for tea and is questioned by Momina and Mariella. Seated are Nene and Clelia.

experience, and we learn more about her.

NENE: I'll have to call home anyway to see if Lorenzo is home yet.

Mariella is arranging her hair in the reflection from the window. Nene is dialling.

MOMINA: Don't do it! My husband, too, always called me supposedly to tell me where he was. Today he sent me the keys for his new apartment in Turin. He has understood that I hate country life.

NENE: Are you going with him?

MOMINA: Perhaps.

MARIELLA: It's been so cosy here. At single women's places, one always thinks that something bad's going on.

Mariella sits on the window sill and pulls the curtain round her shoulder. Momina opens a big box of chocolates and takes out the keys.

MOMINA: He sent them in a box of chocolates. The sweet and the bitter.

NENE: A charming idea.

MOMINA: I'm not supposed to eat any chocolates.

She drops the key back into the box with a gesture, closes it, and replaces it on a side table.

CLELIA: Here's Rosetta.

MOMINA: If only she doesn't make a scene!

Rosetta doesn't make a scene. She apologizes to Clelia and promises to be punctual the next day. Mariella and Momina start questioning her about where she has been, as Mariella has noticed that her blouse is unbuttoned. She goes off into the bathroom to comb her hair. Momina pursues her with questions. The next shots are those described in the extract:

Dance music.

9 In living room looking towards arch leading into bathroom. MS behind Mariella, camera panning left and tracking forward as she walks away from it, and turns round to speak.

MARIELLA: I'm bored.

Camera tracks in to arch, losing Mariella. There is a Venetian blind across the arch. In the background through the blind we see Rosetta's back as she goes into the bathroom from the bedroom, and powders her nose. Momina enters the frame in foreground behind the blind.

MOMINA: Are you following a beauty treatment or are you in love?

ROSETTA: Neither.

Rosetta turns round smiling to face Momina and the camera.

MOMINA: I don't have to be told. I understand now.

ROSETTA: What?

Rosetta goes offscreen right to bedroom, past Momina who follows her, but is still onscreen at cut.

MOMINA: I understood long ago.

---

10 In bedroom looking towards doorway from bathroom. Rosetta comes through door in MS, looking happy, followed by Momina. Pan left with them to include Clelia. They come to stand one on each side of her, Rosetta left, Momina right. Through arch into sitting room we see Nene in ELS.

ROSETTA: What?

CLELIA: What's all the secrecy?

MOMINA (*to Rosetta*): She's found out that you were going to call Lorenzo. And now?

Rosetta waves a finger from side to side and smiles. Momina smiles. Clelia looks at Momina and does not smile.

CLELIA: What are you saying?

MOMINA: Lorenzo.

Rosetta walks away from the other two (pan left with her, losing them and Nene). She turns, leans back against the wall.

CLELIA: Lorenzo!
ROSETTA (*happily*): Lorenzo. Lorenzo.

---

11 As '10' before final pan (MS Clelia and Momina, ELS Nene). Momina walks offscreen right talking. Pan slightly to left as Clelia lets down Venetian blind obscuring Nene, and then pan with her as she walks over to right where Momina is standing in front of a mirror, applying cologne behind her ears.

Momina looks round towards Rosetta who is now behind the camera.

CLELIA: And Nene?
MOMINA: You won't understand. You're not married. If I have an adventure I prefer to tell my husband.
CLELIA: Why?
MOMINA: Because I really love him.

12 Reverse direction looking toward Rosetta in LS picking nightgown off bed. Pan left with her to include the backs of Momina and Clelia at left in foreground. Momina goes over to Rosetta and takes the nightgown. Clelia moves towards them away from the camera. She sits down pensively on bed. Momina and Rosetta have crossed so that Rosetta is back to camera screen left and Momina is facing camera at right.

ROSETTA: Where did you buy this nightgown?

MOMINA: I think Nene isn't indulging in illusions. A woman who is superior to her husband can't be happy.
ROSETTA: Why d'you say that?

13 Rosetta goes across to right and sits on bed. Slight pan with her. Momina now in midscreen strokes Rosetta's hair. Clelia looks fed up. Rosetta lights a cigarette.

Momina walks over to foreground screen left to face the other two (three-quarters back to the camera).
Momina turns away from the other two towards the camera.

MOMINA: You know very well. But the main thing is that you like Lorenzo.
CLELIA: I don't understand you, Momina.
MOMINA: You should know how difficult it is to find the right man. The Prince Charming of today takes dope and dances the mambo. Have fun while you're still young or you'll be sorry when you're old (*the dance music gets louder under her speech*).

Although it's difficult to visualize the actual movement of such a scene from a verbal description, I hope that it may be evident from the extract how the shooting of the scene brings out both its feeling and its implications. I'm thinking particularly of the end of shot '10' where a telling piece of action has been fashioned out of the way Momina, Clelia, and Rosetta each say Lorenzo's name. The pan with Rosetta away from the others allows us to concentrate for a moment on her happiness, and the combination of movements—hers and the camera's—is lyrical in feeling. Notice also the way Nene is in the background except for this moment, and the significance of her handling when we see her again after the cut on Clelia saying 'And Nene?'

After the four shots I've quoted, we are back in the sitting room with Mariella and Nene. They go into the bedroom in time to catch Clelia, who is losing patience with Momina, saying, 'You're wrong,' to her, and then in explanation to them, 'Momina's talking pure nonsense.' Nene borrows a book of matches from Rosetta to light a cigarette. On the flap is a drawing of Rosetta by Lorenzo. We see this in big close-up as Momina's voice says, 'Cesare is ringing.' By linking Nene's realization that Rosetta is Lorenzo's mistress with Momina's announcement of Cesare's arrival, Antonioni is stressing that the two situations are aspects of the same general condition.

Momina and Cesare play their romance by the rules. Momina is happy with this: it's the

Still: Clelia, Nene, Mariella, Momina. Nene asks for a light. Inside the flap of the book matches provided by Rosetta, she will find Lorenzo's drawing.

way she's accustomed to operate—no involvement, no pain. Cesare despises her for her lack of seriousness, just as Clelia despises him. He has a job, although he doesn't take it seriously. He is content to play with Momina. In the last shot of the sequence, taken from outside the house, he is kissing Momina by the window. He notices a man in the yard below and mimes to him to get the hell out. As Momina closes the blinds, the camera tilts down to show the maid opening the side door. She and the man go inside. The poor mimicking the rich.

Back to Clelia and Carlo. She is picking the models for her opening show. Out of jealousy she rejects a girl who flirts with Carlo. Then realizing what she has done she hires the girl.

Lorenzo in a hotel room with Rosetta also has a moment of truth about his romance. Disturbed by the single-mindedness of her passion for him, he says, 'You should have a job that really fills your life.' She replies, 'I'd like to be your wife.' This is given added force by the sordidness of the setting and by a piece of business: Lorenzo opens the door just as a man and a woman come out of a room in the background. He ducks back behind the door. We

realize that he is not prepared to make any sacrifices for Rosetta, that she has deceived herself in thinking he loves her. As they leave, she says, 'I'm fed up with all this secrecy.' Out in the more neutral atmosphere of the street, Lorenzo tries to tell her, as far as his lack of courage will let him, that he is not the ideal man for her. 'I'm a lying coward,' he says. Rosetta ignores his self-deprecation and remarks that she will tell Clelia that she is giving

Still: the fashion show. Above—Mariella (at left) watching the show. Right—Rosetta with Clelia and Nene in the dressing room.

up the salon.

She arrives there as the opening show reaches a successful climax. A wedding dress is shown amid applause, and all the other models come on in evening dress. Nene asks Rosetta to go outside with her. In a corner of the changing

room, surrounded by racks of clothes, Rosetta tells Nene of her love for Lorenzo. 'I don't know if I could ever give him up.' She even manages to convince Nene that Lorenzo loves her. Nene agrees to give Lorenzo up. She will go to America, and Rosetta can tell Lorenzo that he needn't discuss it with her. Setting this scene in a room where models change their clothes suggests the impermanence of sexual relationships in the *milieu* of the film.

Still: the fashion show, Mariella, Nene, Momina.

To celebrate her success, Clelia takes the group out to dinner. They go slumming—to a trattoria in a back street in the sort of district where Clelia grew up. 'Tonight a miracle will happen!' says Mariella. What miracle? 'We'll have fun!' Before they go in, Rosetta tells Lorenzo that she has spoken to Nene. The camera is behind her so that it is his reaction we see. 'You did what?' She walks round a car to face the camera as she explains, 'She started it. She wanted me to tell you that you needn't worry . . . she's going to America.' Rosetta goes off into the trattoria leaving Lorenzo alone in the dark street, facing the camera.

Still: in a corner of the dressing room, Rosetta tells Nene of her love for Lorenzo.

Cesare has picked up an old tramp off the street. Everyone claps in delight at this novelty. The man is given a meal—at a different table. Lorenzo walks past Rosetta and goes over to Nene. As they eat, Cesare does a sketch of Mariella in her wedding dress (she is engaged) and in fun signs it Lorenzo. But Lorenzo gets furious, and when Cesare says 'I'm not joking with society idols who have failed,' he punches him. There is a scuffle. When they have been

Still: in the trattoria—Nene, Rosetta, Lorenzo.

pulled apart, Lorenzo goes out followed by Rosetta. He asks her to leave him alone, but she follows. They stop on a corner in the light of a street lamp. 'I'll always stay with you. You need me.' But Lorenzo rejects her: 'I have to tell you the truth. I don't need anyone.' He moves round the corner into the shadow. Then Rosetta runs away down the street into the distance. A fade closes down. There is a sudden cut from darkness to daylight as a stretcher bearing Rosetta's body, which has just been dragged from the river, is being put into an ambulance. Now the significance of the earlier

shots which connect Rosetta with water is apparent. Antonioni wants us to realize that in the circumstances—social ones—there is no other possible outcome except suicide for Rosetta; that Lorenzo in his failure has no chance of helping her.

Clelia is explaining the tastes of Turin women to her boss when Momina comes in. All Momina can say is 'Who would have thought of it?' Clelia turns on her there in the salon. 'You should have . . . You gave her the key to your apartment . . . You don't know what feelings are . . . You killed her, you and your cynicism.' The customers draw back at this unseemly outburst. One says, 'It doesn't concern us.' But for Antonioni, Rosetta's death as (albeit indirectly) a victim of the system concerns everyone. There is another side to the tragedy—the irony of Rosetta being saved from suicide over Lorenzo at the beginning of the film only to kill herself because of him at the end. This is the final appearance of the old theme of the futility of action affecting others.

Lorenzo returns to Nene. He tries to explain. 'She told me that she loved me and I persuaded myself that I loved her too.' But when he was with her he was always wishing to be with Nene. 'Why do you love me?' he asks her. 'Perhaps because you cost me so much.' For Lorenzo's sake Nene will give up her trip to New York. In this at least the film has moved away from the complete pessimism of *Cronaca* and *Signora* towards *L'Avventura*.

But for Clelia and Carlo, things do not work out. She has arranged to meet him, thinking that she has lost her job. Before he arrives, she sees her boss who offers her the job she had before in Rome as she cannot continue in Turin. A career woman like Clelia, she has used her work as an escape from emotional complications. 'I'm satisfied with myself and above all I've no time to ask myself whether I'm happy or not. Believe me that's the greatest blessing.' Now that she has the choice between Carlo and her job, she cannot face the idea of relative poverty with him. The only way out Antonioni sees for her is working compulsively.

Carlo promises to see her off on the train she has to catch to Rome that evening. Not finding him at the station she phones him. No answer. He is at the station but he does not let her see him as the train leaves. In this lack of courage he is like Guido in *Cronaca*, who says that he will see Paola the next day, although he is going, for good.

Le Amiche, then, has elements of both the earlier and later films. It combines the pessimism of the early ones (Rosetta) with the glimmers of hope which appear later. It is more comprehensive than any of the others in treating the usual subject matter from three angles. Of the three stories, the only one which progresses smoothly is the one which obeys the corrupt conventions of the society in which it takes place. In Momina, we have the most complete expression of Antonioni's hate of the system. The only leading character in his films who has successfully adjusted to the system, she is also the only one who is utterly detestable (to Clelia and the audience, though not perhaps to Antonioni).

Le Amiche is the transition film between the early and late periods in another way: in its structure. Through successive films up to *Il Grido*, there is a reduction in plot and its gradual replacement with a different sort of structure, which is common to the last three films. *Cronaca* is the only one which has a plot in which the external action can be summarized briefly. The minor characters always have a functional place in the plot. *Signora* reduces the neat dovetailing of plot. Instead the film follows a character through a progression of events which lead him or her to a different position at the end. Paola in *Cronaca* had not been changed at all by what happened to her in the film. *Le Amiche* has forsaken plot completely for an interlocking pattern of incidents which is so complex that it is impossible to pick out a story line. All the characters have a significance more important than their contribution to the action. Two, Cesare and Mariella, have no essential effect on what happens to Clelia or to Rosetta. This is a forerunner of the situation in *L'Avventura* where all the minor characters are significant as an environment for the main action, although they hardly take part in it.

With the plot construction has disappeared the irony which was something essentially derived from the plot. In its final appearance in *Le Amiche* it has become rather attenuated compared to the earlier films where it was the main theme. Consequently the feeling of futility has disappeared. Its presence in the early films reflected the mood of much of serious Italian cinema at the start of the 'fifties. With the removal of the one thing which linked him with his contemporaries, Antonioni parted company completely with the rest of the Italian cinema.

The next film, *Il Grido* (1957), is the first one based entirely on the idea of the emotional progression and its physical counterpart, the journey. There is a word which I have been hesitating to use as I shall be accused of drawing unwarranted parallels, although it covers this structure. The word is odyssey. I think, however, that its use here is justified. The situations in which Odysseus was involved along his journey had an effect on his state of mind a significance above that of mere incidents.

Plot engineering never seemed to be much to Antonioni's taste: in the linear structure of the emotional progression journey he seems to have found the ideal vehicle. It is well adapted to his talent: the insistence on giving events their full duration is not conducive to brisk plotmanship.

IL GRIDO

Having found the most effective shape for his films, Antonioni first used it in an unsatisfactory work. The defects of *Il Grido* (*The Outcry*) get in its way very badly, especially on first viewing. Like *Signora* and *I Vinti* and even *La Notte*, it has a seriously flawed surface.

To begin with, Antonioni has gone outside his usual little world again, and failed again in making his characters convincing. In this he is an extremely limited director. It's said that he made a very thorough study of conditions in the Po Valley before starting on *Il Grido*. Certainly that's what it looks like: very accurate but external and lacking life, this in spite of the fact that he spent his childhood there. And if he aimed to deal with immediate social problems, he ended by making a film with slighter social implications than any of the others.

The film was partly American-financed, and suffers a little from having three foreign actors in it. Although he'd handled foreigners very successfully in *Le Amiche* (where Momina and Rosetta are played respectively by British Yvonne Furneaux and German Madeleine Fischer) things turn out less well here: Betsy Blair looks thoroughly out of place, and Steve Cochran is only moderately acceptable. Both, according to Antonioni, were unwilling to accept his usual method of directing actors—telling them what to do but not why they were doing it. The third foreigner, a British former stripper called Lynn Shaw, does excellently.

Il Grido has an atmosphere which is pursued relentlessly and humourlessly throughout the film: it's not tragic, just ever so glum. And the glumness is reinforced by the surroundings—the Po Valley in winter, all bare and muddy. The sameness of the landscape throughout the film reflects the hero's inability to forget. 'The completely open horizon counterpoints the psychology of the central character,' as Antonioni has said. But after a couple of hours one finds oneself adding, 'Who cares?'

Aldo and Irma have been living together in the small town of Goriano for seven years. She has had a child, Rosina, by him. Her husband had left her to go to Australia. At the start of the film she learns from an official that her husband is dead. She takes Aldo his sandwiches but rushes off because she cannot face him. (We do not know yet that she is going to leave him for another and slightly less poor man.) We see Aldo first at his work, for his abandonment of his job and his inability to settle down after he loses Irma provide the subject of the film. He is a skilled hand at a sugar refinery, where he works high up on a tower. Irma bringing his sandwiches is seen from behind him as he stands at the top of the tower. We see the unfriendly countryside all around. He has raised himself up. Soon he will fall.

Aldo learns the news in a very Antonioni way. The good part, her husband's death, comes in the warmth of the kitchen. The conversation is interrupted by Rosina, returning from school. It continues with the bad news out of doors—among a clump of pollarded willow trees with mudflats in the background.

After abortive attempts to make Irma stay with him, Aldo leaves Goriano, taking Rosina, and wanders from place to place, failing to settle down or to forget his unhappiness. Each episode shows this in a different way, and demonstrates the inability of any of the people

Still: the Po valley in winter—Aldo (Steve Cochran) and his daughter, Rosina (Mirna Girardi).

he meets to help him. The characters appear one after another, then are left behind. Aldo is less intelligent than other Antonioni protagonists. He cannot find ways of forgetting as, say, Sandro would. Nor does he have the social distractions available to the others. *Il Grido* is the reverse of *L'Avventura:* a film about Aldo's inability to forget.

After a car trip away from Goriano ('Fine town, Goriano . . . happy people,' comments the driver), and a night in a hotel, where they are disturbed by a boxing match downstairs, Aldo brings Rosina to the home of an old flame of his, Elvira. She lives with her younger sister, Edera, in a large house on the banks of the Po. They have men friends who race hydroplanes. Aldo, who is a skilled mechanic, helps

Still: Aldo with Elvira (Betsy Blair) and her younger sister, Edera (Gabriella Pallotti).

repair one of the hydroplanes for a race. Afterwards on the bank in the rain (of course) Aldo sees Edera having a row with her boy-friend. He walks away from this reminiscent quarrel, followed by Rosina. Irma turns up bringing Aldo's clothes for him while he is out, and talks to Elvira. In the evening the sisters and their friends all go to a dance, and there Elvira tells Aldo that she knows that he wouldn't have come back to her if Irma hadn't left him, that he is only doing it for Rosina. Meanwhile Edera has won a popularity contest. She totters home drunk and tries to seduce Aldo. He and Rosina leave next morning.

Aldo has to reject a job on a remote building site because there is nowhere for Rosina to live. A series of small incidents like this take Aldo's plight and his journey a step further.

One of the lifts which they hitch on their journey ends at a roadside gas station. Its owner is a blousy young woman called Virginia (how convenient it is that no two characters in Antonioni's black and white movies have the same first name). With her lives her senile father. As Aldo and Rosina arrive, Virginia and two policemen are bringing back father, who keeps running away. Because Aldo helps Virginia with the pumps, she lets him stay the night with Rosina in an outhouse, and then offers him a job. He stays on, and becomes her lover. Rosina teams up with the old man, and goes with him when he makes trouble with neighbours who live on the farm that was his until Virginia sold it to buy the gas station. He is relevant to Aldo's situation as a man who has lost his work and because of that, his grip on life. Virginia wants to get rid of him and of Rosina, both burdens she is unwilling to accept. The old man is packed off to a home.

After they have disposed of him, they wander round the town. Aldo nearly gets into a fight. Rosina runs off. We next see her asleep on a piece of waste land just outside the town. The ground is strewn with big cable reels. Aldo and Virginia go around to the other side of them, spread their coats on the ground and sit down. Meanwhile Rosina wakes up and starts playing a little game of collecting pebbles. The camera is on the same side as Aldo and Virginia when Rosina starts looking among the reels, and comes through between them into medium shot. She stares towards the couple on the ground offscreen, and then backs away, dropping the pebbles one by one. Virginia insists that she couldn't have understood. All Aldo can say is 'Irma.'

So Rosina has to be sent back to Goriano. By now she isn't speaking to Aldo. As her bus moves off, Aldo runs beside it trying despairingly to explain things to her. Without Rosina, he can't face life with Virginia. He goes into the café where she is waiting, looks over towards her and leaves without a word.

He takes a job on a dredger. With another member of the crew he talks of escape to South America, encouraged by the captain of the boat who paints a rosy picture of life there.

But escape is no solution. Aldo takes up with another girl, this time as poor as he is. Andreina works in the rice fields in the summer and just manages to keep alive by a bit of prostitution in the winter. We have already seen her going off with the captain of the dredger. Aldo passes her hut when she is sick with malaria. He gets a doctor and forces him to attend to her. But later he sees a couple of policemen passing, takes fright and runs off. When Andreina recovers she goes to find him and return the donkey jacket which he had lent to her. He is unemployed, living in a rush hut on a mudflat and eating only the coarse fish he is able to catch. She stays with him.

Andreina is a much more generous girl than Virginia, but Aldo is so sunk in his memories that he never manages to communicate with her. He tells her how he met Irma. They are standing on a mudflat which recalls the one in the background when he learned Irma was leaving him. It is completely bare except for a couple of decoy ducks sitting incongruously in the middle. The actors are seen either in disjointed long shots or alone in medium shot to emphasize their separation. While Aldo talks about meeting Irma, Andreina is playing with one of the ducks. 'Then what?' although she's not really interested. 'I had a good job at the refinery, with responsibility. I worked high up. I could see my daughter playing.' 'I was pregnant once,' she remarks with an apparent lack of connection: conversations in Antonioni often turn into counterpointing monologues.

They have no work and no money. The local shopkeeper will only sell food for cash. The man who is sharing the hut with them goes home to his brother. When the Po floods after the spring thaw, the hut will be submerged. Already rain is pouring through the roof. Unable to stand her hunger any longer Andreina sneaks off to get a meal by sleeping with a café owner. Aldo follows her. He stands outside the café shouting her name until she comes out. When he objects to what she's doing, she bawls him out. She relents too late, he has walked off. She is still sobbing when the fat owner comes downstairs. 'You can go to hell too,' she says, and goes out.

Fade-in to Aldo on a truck approaching Virginia's gas station from the opposite direction to that of the tanker before. Virginia has a coat over her dressing-gown. She asks him, 'Still looking for a job? Or something else? Not worn out yet?' When he's inside collecting his suitcase he sees Virginia's father who has been thrown out of the home because he kept on escaping. Virginia remembers that there was a card from Irma for Aldo. She thinks it was about Rosina, but she's lost it and can't tell him what it said. The camera is on the truck with Aldo as it drives off, and Virginia recedes into the distance. She is left behind just as Aldo leaves everything in the film, except his misery.

When the truck reaches the outskirts of Goriano it is diverted by police. Aldo gets off. The road into town is closed because of a riot. He walks into town, breaking through crowds demonstrating against a proposed American airbase which will put peasants off their land. We see the workers in the sugar refinery leaving to join the demonstration. In the deserted town Aldo notices Rosina going into a house. He peers in through the window and sees Irma powdering a young baby. She catches sight of him; she goes out after him. He finds an open gate into the refinery, and goes in. Irma sees him climb up the tower to where he once worked. She calls out to him. Then things turn ambiguous—not usefully ambiguous, just unclear. He starts to sway and then falls to the ground. It looks like vertigo, but that seems a pointless ending, so presumably it's suicide. The last high-angle shot shows demonstrators running in the distance and tilts down to Irma kneeling over Aldo's body.

The personal/political linkage which is intended between the destruction of Aldo and the destruction of Goriano's whole way of life seems terribly forced, partly perhaps because the film and its hero have become such a bore that we have lost sympathy. Along its length there are a few good and meaningful scenes like the ones I've described, and a number of nicely calculated incidents. Example: to impose his will on her Aldo grabs Irma's arm as she is putting on Rosina's milk to warm and succeeds only in making her drop the saucepan. She asks, 'Now what'll I give Rosina?' But elsewhere it is a drag—not that it aspires to the monumental tedium of *La Terra Trema*, just that it seems to communicate less than any other Antonioni film, even perhaps *I Vinti*.

Still: Virginia (Dorian Gray) and Aldo.

L'AVVENTURA

Having tried to explain how almost everything which people cheered or detested in *L'Avventura* was present in the earlier films, I'm left with the simpler task of writing about why it looks different from its predecessors. There are, I think, two main reasons for the difference: one personal, one technical.

The personal reason is the appearance of hope in Antonioni's picture of the world. Although he had already lost the obsession with futility which pervades the early films, in *Il Grido* he is more consistently gloomy than in any of the others. At least Paola and Clara and Rosetta had some good times before things went wrong. In *Il Grido* these are all over before the picture starts. At the end of *L'Avventura* there is hope; that Claudia and Sandro will stay together, and that Sandro will, after his moment of truth, be able to work up the strength necessary to drop his degrading but lucrative work for Ettore and practise again as an architect. If I were a gossip columnist, I would attribute this new tentative optimism to the arrival of Monica Vitti in Antonioni's life.

The technical advance in *L'Avventura* is very simple: it is the wide screen. *L'Avventura* is in a screen ratio of 1.85, I'd guess, from a couple of viewings in ideal conditions. The new shape has allowed Antonioni to get much closer to his characters without losing anything important. On a normal screen, a shot containing two or more people just standing and talking will necessarily include a lot of their bodies and thus have the faces appearing quite small on the screen. The distance at which this places the actors is bad in *Il Grido* and perhaps worse in parts of *Signora*, although what's happening there is more interesting in compensation. *Signora* has almost no cutting and approaches a one-take-per-scene technique, which Antonioni has increasingly replaced by cutting. In *L'Avventura* the two-shots have the actors' faces as large on the screen as they would be in a medium close-up on a normal screen. This is important for Antonioni who relies so heavily on our observations of the characters' behaviour. We can be close to them without having them isolated from each other and the background in a close-up. *Le Amiche*, incidentally, solved the problem in rather a different way, by shooting group scenes on more than one level, with the characters standing on a slope or some standing, some sitting, to produce a sort of vertical depth of field.

Apart from the optimism and the wide screen, *L'Avventura* does have very close antecedents in the early pictures. It is, as Antonioni remarked, *Il Grido delle Amiche*. From *Le Amiche* come many of the characters—one can trace parallels to various extents between Claudia and Clelia, Anna and Rosetta, Sandro and Lorenzo (both played by Ferzetti, too), Giulia and Momina, Ettore and Cesare. From *Il Grido* comes the journey structure, although this time it is used to greater effect. The surroundings shape the events. The island, barren and unfriendly, breaks up relationships, isolates the characters from each other. The journey in train and car brings the changes in Sandro and Claudia; the places they pass through are not merely a reflection of what is happening inside them, they help to cause it. The big hotel, home of the rich, weakens, even corrupts Sandro. The dawn signifies the end of the destructive night, the beginning of something new. The bare, cold car park is an escape from the warm, ornate corruption of the hotel, the emptiness in which a different and perhaps better future can be created. The car park is less attractive, less inviting than the hotel, but is the alternative which offers hope. For the first time, Antonioni's characters have found a conclusion that does not imply defeat and renunciation, but expresses mutual shame and forgiveness, and therefore contains the possibility of progress.

Stills: L'Avventura *has a set of leading characters parallel to that in* Le Amiche. *Right—Giulia (Dominique Blanchar). Below—Claudia (Monica Vitti).*

LA NOTTE

La Notte is an attempt to go beyond what was achieved in *L'Avventura*. In fact, I don't think that anyone who hasn't seen *L'Avventura* has much chance of understanding it.

La Notte starts with hope. The first shot tilts up from the overcrowded streets of Milan in the rush hour to the tall Pirelli building. The cool beauty of Gio Ponti's architecture is an image of the possible future environment, a triumph of art and science working together. It embodies a perfection to which man in his personal relationships can only aspire. But here it is, rising out of the traffic jams and the confusion. A couple of coldish shots along the top of the building remind us that better does not mean more lush—we learned that at the end of *L'Avventura*. Then under the titles, down we go, in two of the longest vertical travelling shots ever seen, toward the chaotic present. At first we see the rest of Milan only as a reflection: then a different angle includes a direct view as well. This credit sequence goes beyond the plain fact of change presented at the beginning of *L'Avventura*. ('These new flats will stifle our poor villa,' says Anna's father.) The change is potentially for the better. Significantly, though, the Pirelli building is the only piece of good modern architecture in the film.

In *La Notte* we are shown another progression, again of a couple, Lidia and Giovanni. But this time the testing point in their relationship comes after ten years of marriage. As in *L'Avventura*, their personal crisis is linked with another crisis, in Giovanni's work—he is a novelist.

The action is compressed into less than 24 hours—Saturday afternoon to early Sunday morning. Perhaps this is a reaction to accusations of diffuseness in Antonioni's previous films. However, it does take the idea that the duration of events is important a stage further by representing a smaller section of time more completely.

The visit to their dying friend Tommaso, which forms the opening section of the film, is the trigger to the estrangement between Lidia and Giovanni. Or rather, it helps to bring out into the open a situation which has already grown up unacknowledged. We learn that all is not well between them as they go up to Tommaso's room. The camera is inside the lift so that we see them coming in from the foyer of the clinic (a modern building which 'evokes the idea of a perfect and inexorable science'). The script (the published version written after the film, not by Antonioni) describes it like this:

In the lift which goes up without any vibration and with hardly even a slight hum, Giovanni and Lidia avoid looking at each other. It is an unpleasant moment, made even more painful by the surroundings and the decor. Lidia looks at the ceiling, Giovanni at the control panel. Then the hum stops and the gate opens automatically.

Tommaso, as a failure (a critic or columnist of some sort), in the extreme situation of knowing he's about to die, is forced to reconsider his life. 'I realized how many things I'd left undone. . . . I began to ask myself if I hadn't stayed on the fringe of an undertaking that concerned me. . . . I didn't have the courage to get to the root of things. . . . And very often I consoled myself by saying that I didn't have the intelligence.' Giovanni interrupts him—'If you talk like that there'll be nothing left for me to do but to stop writing, and look straight away for a good job. . . . But you're only saying it in fun.' Giovanni feels that what Tommaso says is equally applicable to himself. (A recurrent motif in Antonioni is characters seeing themselves in others: the audience can do the same. When Tommaso talks of failure, to Giovanni it's his failure.)

Tommaso's desperate desire to be close to

Still: Lidia (Jeanne Moreau) and Giovanni (Marcello Mastroianni) visit their dying friend Tommaso (Bernhard Wicki).

them (twice he says that they are his only friends) points their avoidance of contact with him and each other. Instead, both of them make a display of solicitousness, which keeps them at a distance from him. Giovanni brushes aside Tommaso's references to his new novel which has just been published. Lidia stands behind the head of the bed, where Tommaso cannot see her. Shots of her tend to include the view out the window. When a helicopter passes, she

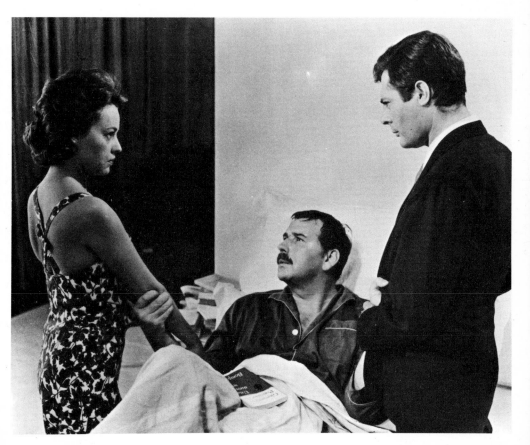

rushes over to the window to look out at it.
Seeing Tommaso have a stab of pain, she hastily
offers to get a nurse. All the time it's obvious to
us that she really wants to escape.

The framing of the shots carries the idea of
the couple's estrangement by frequently showing Tommaso in two-shot with just one of them.
On one occasion when he is in pain, they each
hold one of his hands. He is between and linking
them.

*Still: Giovanni opens the champagne which
Tommaso's clinic provides.*

Even Tommaso becomes aware of how they
feel about him. He is annoyed when Giovanni
talks of him getting better. 'Treat me as a
friend, not as an invalid. I know very well how
this is going to end.'

This first scene contains in outline most of
the themes that are developed later in the film.

The place of the artist in modern society. The crisis in Giovanni's career and in Lidia's marriage with him. The corruption of the benefits of life in a scientific age when they are placed at the service of a capitalist society. Champagne for the dying rich, beautiful nurses to keep up their morale. These images suggest a dying society and culture which are being kept alive artificially.

Outside the clinic, Lidia weeps convulsively. She is leaning against a wall. Her posture demonstrates her emotional need for support. In the clinic Giovanni has his encounter with the nymphomaniac. She asks him for a match. Antonioni cuts from LS to a single shot of Giovanni. Behind him the elevator doors close, cutting off his retreat. Very corny. Giovanni, completely drained of resistance, allows himself to be dragged into the nympho's room. She is completely oblivious of whether he is aroused at all. Suddenly he comes to life and returns her caresses with as much intensity as he can muster (much less than she can, because he's Marcello Mastroianni). There is a link between her and Lidia, expressed visually in the shot of her against the screen-filling expanse of bare wall. Giovanni feels, wrongly, that he has excited in her the passion that he can no longer produce in Lidia. Unlike Lidia, all she needs is the physical presence of a man, any man. It's only when the nurses come in and slap the girl's face to stop her hysteria that Giovanni understands what had happened.

The drive from the clinic to the publishing house, which is holding a reception to launch Giovanni's new book, starts with a very lengthy silent shot taken through the windshield of the car. Giovanni repeatedly looks round at Lidia, trying to bring himself to speak. It's obvious that he can't keep silent for long about what has happened, but first he needs to muster his courage. For her part, Lidia stares straight ahead miserably, only glancing at him once.

We are aware of the gap between them, and the length of the take allows us to experience the duration of the silence, to feel their isolation building up as they are unable to speak to each other.

The car runs into a traffic jam, of which we're shown a few documentary shots. The jam has two functions: one is a reference back to the shot which opens the titles sequence—the confusion of the present; the other has to do with the journey that's in progress. The movement

Still: Giovanni and the nympho (Maria Pia Luzi).

of the car reflects the way in which the emotional changes are progressing. On the whole, the things which are pushing them apart take place when the car is moving: the silence, for example. The car stops. Giovanni puts his hand on Lidia's knee (high shot showing only her and his hand). This is the physical evidence that he's trying to re-establish contact. He asks her if she's not too tired to go to the reception. He has to tell her something she won't like. She asks, 'Do you really have to?' He is just launching into his story. Lidia says, 'What girl?' The traffic starts moving. As they drive slowly he tells her what

Still: Lidia and Giovanni.

happened. She is as calm as he is agitated. When they have to stop again, she asks why he called the incident unpleasant. He explains that he thought for a moment that he was the cause of the girl's passion. Now Lidia is nervous. The car starts moving again. She is sufficiently upset to make absolutely the wrong remark—'It's always an experience. Good material for a novel, *The Living and the Dead*.' Giovanni is hurt by her unconcern. 'Is that all you can say?'

The emotional gap has widened further, and

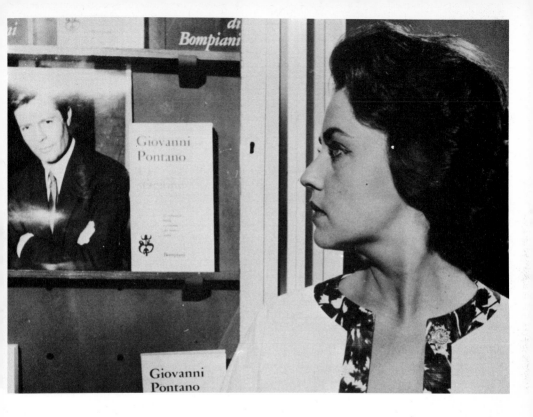

the rest of the scene, as the car continues on its way, is accordingly either shot from behind them for two-shots or in single-shots—not close-ups. Some people have the impression that Antonioni used lots of close-ups to get even nearer to his actors than in *L'Avventura*. This is not true. Most of the single shots aren't any closer than the two-shots in *L'Avventura*. Their function is the separation of the characters from each other to parallel their emotional isolation.

Lidia is distressed by her unfortunate remark, for she tries to make light of the incident. 'That girl's the lucky one . . . because she's not

Still: Lidia at the press reception for Giovanni's book.

responsible.' Her last remark before the car draws up at the publisher's is: 'It hasn't changed anything. . . . Don't worry.' That is the truth: her feelings for her husband have ebbed so far that she is not jealous of his near-infidelity. This theme reappears more strongly at the end of the film.

The reception shows us a little of what Giovanni has achieved by his writing. We already know that he hasn't made a vast amount of money (his car is neither large nor new), although he's doing quite well financially (both he and Lidia are well dressed). Giovanni has had a modest, but fashionable, success, and this cocktail party is evidence of how good he is at being a success.

For Giovanni this is the reward for his work: silly questions ('I see you always sign at the left . . .'), mechanical smiles and handshakes. The book is called *La Stagione*, The Season: something else that is transient. Lidia looks at a big picture of Giovanni in a display case (which is metaphorically where he is at the time) beside his novel. She feels outside everything that is happening in the room and not concerned in her husband's success. She watches a couple of girls come in. One says, 'I'd love to write a novel.' The last shot of the sequence looks down on a table as Lidia pushes her arm between the backs of two separate groups of people to put her drink down.

Instead of going home, she wanders around. We see her stop to stare at a car park attendant who is leaning against a wall, eating his sandwiches. As she walks off he notices her and stares after her. She turns and smiles at him. She passes a couple of men who are walking in the opposite direction and joking. For a moment she shares their laughter. From our observations of her behaviour we sense that she is trying to overcome her feeling of isolation, not only from Giovanni, but from people in general.

She walks along a street of dull and rather inhuman new flats. An extreme long shot shows that next to the flats is an old and partly demolished slum building. The town-proud materialists have had it screened from the road by an advertisement hoarding covered with Omo posters. Lidia finds a door in the hoarding and enters, escaping from the present and her loneliness (represented by the impersonal coldness of the flats) into the past which looks more friendly. In the yard of the old building, she

tries to comfort a crying child, but without success. She wanders back towards the door, looking at things, and touching them as if unsure of the reality of the world she is moving in. The symbolism here is pushed a little too hard in a couple of close shots: her feet beside a broken old clock lying on the ground; her left hand, with wedding ring, pulling a large flake of rust off an iron door. As Lidia walks back into the present, we return to Giovanni who is arriving home.

Alone in his study, Giovanni acts out his state of mind. He pulls a sheet of paper out of his typewriter, reads it and drops it on his desk. Then he leans back in his seat looking glum, because his writing has become stale. He gets up and paces around the room, picking up a cutting to glance at it, then going over to the window to stare out. This is a delaying action. He doesn't want to settle down to work. Finally he lies down on a couch to read his mail.

Back to Lidia: a high-angle extreme long shot of her appearing round a corner. Most of the screen is filled by an expanse of plain mosaic wall, stressing the coldness of the architecture which makes her feel a stranger to her surroundings. A closer shot shows her against the wall, looking around her. The sudden noise of a jet accentuates her feelings of fear at being so completely alone. It is a hot Saturday afternoon and the street is deserted. She walks past the entrance hall of the block and looks in at the porter. When he notices her, she walks away.

Part of Lidia's problem is sexual, and during the first half of the film, phallic symbols keep popping up. The champagne bottle in the Tommaso sequence was one. Later there are the rockets. The most blatant of all comes at this point in the film. Lidia threads her way along a row of concrete posts, absently fingering the first few. A tracking shot just above shoulder level behind her leaves us in no doubt of their significance. After she has passed two or three, her little game is stopped by an old woman who is eating her lunch off one. The camera cranes down to a more normal angle and tilts up as she walks away.

The tilt up is countered by a tilt down to the street with Lidia and the camera a hundred yards further down the street in front of one more horrid modern block of flats. A low-angle shot makes us feel the weight of the buildings oppressing her. She leans against a lamp-post for support. This is perhaps the first time that Antonioni ever made one of his characters act in a way that appears false in order to produce a meaningful shot.

A cut from the no-sky claustrophobia of this shot takes us to the open landscape of the edge of town as Lidia arrives in a taxi. A few large sheds and occasional houses alternate with patches of wasteland covered in rubble and obviously destined soon to be built on: an area of change. On to one piece of wasteland troop a gaggle of tough young men. One removes his shirt and after a formal exchange of insults with another starts a fist fight. Lidia is hypnotised by the violence (as Giovanni was in the scene with the nymphomaniac). Her expression betrays sexual desire, but with her genteel background she can't help also being repelled. Eventually she cries 'Basta' until they stop. The victor gets up. While he puts his shirt on, he looks her over with a defiant leer. She walks off, but breaks into a run as he starts to follow. Like Giovanni with the nymphomaniac, Lidia has realized what was happening.

No sooner is she back at the taxi than she sees some young men in the distance setting off rockets. Her need to be with people makes her join the small crowd who are watching. The sight does not detain her for long. Once more she wanders off.

At home, Giovanni, who has dropped off to sleep, wakes up with a start and calls Lidia.

She's not in. He asks their neighbour, but she hasn't seen Lidia for two days. He picks up the phone, thinks better of it and wanders out on to the balcony. A long shot of the block. In comparison he's so minute that our eyes have to search around the screen before we spot him. A shot from behind him along the balcony showing a man looking out of his window in the next block. A rather closer shot of the man, who just smokes and stares out at Giovanni. Antonioni's comment on urban life: everyone filed away in his own pigeon-hole, out of touch with people in the surrounding pigeon-holes. This in itself links to Lidia's essentially urban problem of outsideness.

The phone rings. It's Lidia who is now at an open air café. It is a place where the couple used to meet before they were married. So, as in Le Amiche, we have a journey back to the past in an attempt to recapture something lost. We get an indication that this is wrong from the café owner who comes up to Lidia and says, 'There's a hotel nearby if you're meeting anyone. . . .' She is a very fat middle-aged woman grotesquely dressed in girlish clothes. Like the visit to Tommaso the scene will bring out only their separation.

Lidia goes through a gate into a courtyard more shots of old buildings. Giovanni arrives. 'Why come here?' he asks. 'By chance, perhaps.' Again single shots of them expressing isolation, and one in which he walks away from her, the camera tracking with him to leave her in the background. The excuse for calling him was to see the rockets. 'The way they go up, it's so pretty.' But the launching has stopped.

Giovanni, who is the less aware of the alteration in their relationship, says 'It looks all unchanged.' Lidia adds 'It will, and soon.' Change, for the Antonioni of this period, is the one certainty. It is because Lidia recognizes one change that she suffers more than Giovanni, and is the dominant character in the film. Antonioni has

Stills: Lidia, Giovanni and (right) a use for sculpture.

said, 'It seems to me that female psychology is a finer filter for reality than male psychology. Anyway, women are less hypocritical by nature than men, therefore more interesting.'

Lidia and Giovanni walk across an overgrown railway line. He says, 'These rails were in use when we came here.' And that again is a comment on the decay of their relationship.

Lidia in the bath calls to Giovanni to pass her the sponge. In a naturally offhand way, he picks it out of the washbasin, gives it to her and goes out. The shot of her is held; we only see the lower part of him as his is a casual action. Lidia is upset by the lack of attention. She talks to him as he dresses in another room. She's bored with staying at home. 'Let's go to the Gherardinis,' he shouts. 'Whatever you like, but don't let's stay at home.' Giovanni doesn't know what Gherardini wants with him. Lidia guesses correctly: 'Every millionaire wants his intellectual. He's chosen you.'

While they talk she makes some display of drying herself. But he doesn't notice as he's accustomed to seeing her naked and the fact of her nakedness has ceased to mean anything.

She comes out of the bathroom wearing a new dress, and does a fashion-model walk down the hall for Giovanni's benefit. He notices the dress, but not her. She turns around to look at him, and the smile drains from her face. He asks, 'What's the matter?' But she can't tell him. Instead she manoeuvres to get him closer. 'Do me up.' While fastening her dress he puts down his whisky glass on a handy piece of abstract sculpture. The degradation of art theme again. She has now decided not to go to the Gherardinis'. 'Somewhere else. . . . I'd prefer to be with just you.' He kisses her on the neck. 'Perhaps that would be better.' She turns, hoping to capitalize on the intimacy of the moment, but he has picked up his glass and is out of reach.

The night-club act is another piece of modern grotesqueness—a combination balancing/contortionist/striptease number which recalls the eroticism theme of *L'Avventura*. It seems to interest Giovanni in a way that the sight of Lidia in the bath did not. However, by fixing his attention on it, he is avoiding her gaze which is centred on him. She notices this: 'Watching you can be very amusing . . . when you're with me you seem to be acting.' Giovanni is not going to be led into conversation.

'Look at her, she's not bad.' To emphasize the break, there is a cut to the performers with Giovanni and Lidia in the background. We see that the act is done with much skill, but absolutely no grace. A close shot over her shoulder as she sips her drink, then puts her glass down. She runs her hand over the jewelled clip of her handbag and then touches Giovanni's cuff links. She smiles privately at him. According to the script, the cuff-links have the same stone in the same mounting as her engagement ring. Giovanni acts exasperation at being distracted from the floorshow. Again Lidia expresses her need

for Giovanni to value her more—'Don't minimize my capabilities. I have thoughts too.' In their mutual discomfort this is turned to a joke as she describes the arrival of a thought. More floorshow. When the thought has arrived, she will not say what it is, only that it is not pleasant. Her gesture of straightening his collar is filled with tenderness she still feels for him.

But the evening together has failed to bring Giovanni closer to her again. She suggests that they go to the Gherardinis'. She has changed her mind because 'It gives us something to do.' The trip to the suburbs, the bath scene and the night club were her attempts to break down the barrier that had grown up between them. The party is going to be what the night club already is for him—an external distraction which will cover up the trouble. They perceive different facets of the same crisis: Lidia is the more sensitive to her failure in rebuilding their relationship, Giovanni to the stalemate in his career. This is brought into the nightclub sequence when Giovanni says, 'Life would be tolerable but for its pleasures.' 'Original?' 'No, I no longer have ideas—just a good memory.' The visit to Gherardini, the millionaire who wants to buy Giovanni as his tame intellectual, is, then, their unconscious acknowledgment of their double failure.

The rest of the film takes place in and around the Gherardinis' house. It is as characteristic of the upper strata of capitalism as the hotel in *L'Avventura*. Architecturally it's undistinguished—the sort of diffuse luxury that any puppet architect would produce for a rich client with slightly 'modern' ideas. From the house a wide lawn slopes gently down towards a swimming pool and a circular dance floor which surrounds a statue of a laughing satyr. Nearby a quartet plays soggy modern jazz. A row of tables are loaded with an opulent buffet far in excess of the potential consumption of the guests.

At first the party succeeds in its function as a distraction for Lidia and Giovanni. Accordingly we too are distracted from them and our attention is first switched to the house and some of the people at the party. There's Berenice, a raddled, neurotic woman in her middle thirties. She's Anna from *L'Avventura* ten years later.

Another of the guests is a solid-looking blonde girl called Resy (short for Maria Teresa). Constantly needing people around to divert her (a more permanent version of Lidia's trouble of the afternoon), she seizes on Giovanni as some-

one to idolize. She wants him to tell her a lovely story about a beautiful woman who is loved for her intelligence. But how could it end? Resy goes for self-sacrifice: her heroine would give up her lover to another woman. Giovanni is still sufficient of a writer to ask 'Why does she give him up?' But Resy prefers self-indulgence: 'Because it makes me want to cry.'

Having failed in her attempt to get through to Giovanni, Lidia is now avoiding contact with other people. She refuses to let Berenice introduce her to a playboy friend, Roberto, and even uses his arrival to escape from her. Wandering through the house, she comes on Gherardini's daughter Valentina sitting alone on a staircase reading a vast egghead volume *I Sonnambuli*. At this point we're not shown Valentina's face but merely made aware of her presence.

It's Lidia who first mentions her to Giovanni, to dodge the issue when he says 'You never seem to enjoy yourself any longer.' 'I do in my way,' she replies. 'There's a girl inside who's enjoying herself in her way. . . . She's reading *I Sonnambuli*, and she's very beautiful.' This remark, however strange it may seem, in the circumstances has no deeper motivation than the avoidance of an argument.

Seeing the Gherardinis approach, Lidia tries to escape only to be turned back to them by the sight of Roberto on the prowl. The whole conversation with Gherardini is given a particular sort of ludicrousness by its setting. Having seen his house and its grounds, we are hardly sympathetic to his opening gambit. 'It's absurd to talk of wealth these days. The rich no longer exist.' One feels that one is hearing a well-rehearsed sale talk. 'I have always regarded my many enterprises as works of art, and I can say that the money I make . . . it's as if it doesn't concern me.' Through the character of Gherardini, we are shown the hypocrisy of the liberal capitalist. His attitude seems utterly self-centred when he says, 'What's important for me is to create something solid to live on after me.' The more he says, the sillier and more high-flown becomes the parallel he draws between Giovanni's work and his own. 'Believe me, we are the sole architects of our lives. What would you do, Pontano, if you didn't write?'

Giovanni's crisis is mentioned directly for the first time in the film by Lidia: 'A few years ago he would have committed suicide. But now . . . you should know, Giovanni. . . .' And so we learn more about the nature of his trouble which is partly a feeling that there is no place for him in a technological society. 'I don't give myself that much importance. There are other ways out. [One of which Gherardini later offers him.] Today a writer asks himself all the time if his vocation isn't a reflex that's—irrepressible, certainly, but almost anachronistic. . . . You industrialists have the advantage of constructing your stories with real people, real houses, real towns. The rhythm of life and even that of time are in your hands.' This is put in its proper perspective by Lidia: 'It's been a particularly bad day.' Giovanni's questioning of his vocation is not separate from the rest of his life.

Gherardini's wife keeps interrupting her husband's monologue, much to his annoyance. Unlike most of the idle rich, she doesn't seem to be either a neurotic or an all-out hedonist. Her intelligence, of which she's obviously proud, is devoted rather endearingly to deflating her husband's pomposity. When she's had enough of the conversation, she leads Lidia off, leaving him saying 'Perhaps all our privileges will be swept away, but that will be a good thing. Yes, a good thing.'

If Gherardini and his wife are rather different from any previous Antonioni characters, their daughter Valentina is quite without antecedents in his films. Her character breaks refreshingly across all the assumptions that were becoming dangerously consistent in the other films: that wealth was incompatible with self-awareness and ideas of responsibility to other people.

It's relevant that we see her first playing a game she has invented (with her compact on the checkered tile floor). So too is what would have seemed at the time to be the admirable intellectual preciseness of the MJQ record she's playing, in contrast to the flatulent jazz that's going on outside. The game is a metaphor representing her whole life. (In another scene she says 'I'm just a girl who loves golf, tennis, cars, cocktails.') A game in which she makes the rules, but is involved wholeheartedly so that the result is serious:

VALENTINA: To win, you have to make the compact stop in one of those squares. The end row.

GIOVANNI: What's the prize?

VALENTINA: We'll think what we'd like and ask for it at the end of the game. I'm called Valentina.

GIOVANNI: Valentina . . . do you often lose at this game?

VALENTINA: I've only just invented it. . . . Once I lost everything.

Within the context of the game Valentina's character begins to be established. When other guests gather round and start betting on the players, Giovanni is upset by the size of the stakes. Valentina picks on his weakness: 'You're worried about the losers . . . a typical intellectual attitude . . . an egoist with a bleeding heart.'

The next scene between Giovanni and Valentina shows us a little more of her and him a little more of himself.

GIOVANNI: There's one way of bringing us closer . . .

VALENTINA: You crave affection?

GIOVANNI: You don't?

Silence. They look at each other. Giovanni starts again.

GIOVANNI: You know, I owe you a debt. Just

85

now I gave up.

VALENTINA: Give me a little more time to relish the idea of this debt.

GIOVANNI: Agreed . . . but don't forget.

Valentina, who was moving away, stops.

VALENTINA: Each day I seem to forget something.

Instead of answering Giovanni kisses her gently.

From a medium shot Antonioni cuts to a high-angle shot including Lidia who is looking down at them.

We have reached the climax of the film, not that any scene is built up emotionally as a coda. In the rest of the film various themes are brought together. Antonioni's method is exposition rather than dramatisation. After the game, incidents happen in this order: (1) Lidia avoids Roberto. (2) She phones the clinic and learns of Tommaso's death. (3) She sees Giovanni kiss Valentina. (4) Giovanni is offered a job by Gherardini. (5) Valentina finds out that Lidia

is Giovanni's wife. (6) Lidia tries to talk to Giovanni, but he rushes off after Valentina. (7) When it starts raining and guests jump into the pool, Roberto stops Lidia from jumping and bundles her into his car.

These seven incidents show the destruction of what little is left of the couple's relationship, leading up to the moment when Lidia is unable to resist Roberto. The order in which they happen is meaningful because sequences are linked together in significance by their juxtaposition. For example, (2), (3), and (4): the death of Tommaso (their shared past); Lidia seeing Giovanni kiss Valentina (his first voluntary attempt at infidelity); Gherardini's offer (which would mean the abandonment of Giovanni's vocation). In an even more complex way this recalls the hotel scene of *L'Avventura* where Sandro betrays his vocation and Claudia with Ettore and Gloria respectively.

Giovanni's conversation with Gherardini

Stills: Valentina's game; Roberto stops Lidia jumping in the pool; Valentina and Lidia.

shows us more of the millionaire's brand of paternal capitalism, and makes it very clear that if Giovanni works for him, his job will be even less rewarding than Sandro's estimating. 'I have started a cultural programme for my employees. I wish to rejuvenate the spirit of my firm. I have noticed a lack of *rapport* between the management and the workers. And do you know why? Because they don't know the story of the firm and of me, its founder.' Gherardini's materialism penetrates his whole life. (Earlier, showing his roses to a guest—'Over there are more than three thousand rose bushes.') So it's hardly surprising that it comes out in his view of culture. The whole cultural project is no more than Industrial (and Public) Relations. He backs up his explanation with a diagram which he draws on a sheet of paper with decisive strokes. A managerial gimmick if ever there was one, it demonstrates nothing. He wants Giovanni to write a history of his firm, 'but

that's not all, I also want you as one of our directors. Wouldn't that please you: to work here, to live as we live? Excuse me, but what do you earn now? . . . Your wife's family is wealthy isn't it?' While he is talking, Gherardini scrawls a row of o's on his paper, ready to put a number in front of them when he names his price. Giovanni is beginning to be sales-resistant: 'You're well informed, but you've missed that I have means of my own . . . and then, I write a lot of articles for the papers.' Gherardini's next remark is quite astounding, although he would not see that it was in any way extraordinary: 'Don't you want independ-ence?' Giovanni immediately questions it: 'In-dependence, by what definition?' That is not the sort of remark that Gherardini condescends to notice. 'Think it over, Pontano, think it over,

87

and remember that in my firm, I pay top salaries as a matter of policy.' There's a meaningful cut straight from this to his wife's hitching up her skirt to show some guests a combined garter and billfold, complete with dollar bill. An onlooker makes a crack about extending the dollar area.

Valentina's look of disgust at this exhibition turns to one of horror when her mother calls to Lidia who's standing on a balcony. (One of the recurrent visual motifs in the party is Lidia looking down on the others, particularly Valentina and Roberto, as if at a distance from everything that affects her.) The blow to Valentina in learning that Giovanni is married has its counterpart for Lidia when she tries to tell him about Tommaso's death and fails because he's chasing after Valentina. He comes on Lidia sitting alone during his search for Valentina. 'Beautiful here, isn't it?' He sees Valentina in the distance and starts after her before Lidia has pulled herself together enough to say urgently, 'Giovanni!' All she gets for an answer is: 'I'll be back in a moment.'

Giovanni's refusal to listen has left Lidia even more desolate, without any will of her own. Leaning against the piano on the lawn, she lets herself be taken up by the rhythm of the music. Soon her conscious misery has gone, although underneath the emptiness remains. When a man asks her to dance with him, she does, only to find that he can't dance. At this, she even manages a wan smile as she dances a moment alone.

When the rain scatters the dancers, one girl is left embracing the stone satyr in the middle of the dance floor. Some of the others rush down to the water and jump in—one is reminded irresistibly of the Gadarene swine. Lidia finds it all amusing. She's up on the spring board and about to jump too, when Roberto stops her. This is the last time she is seen above the others. She does not resist as

Roberto leads her to his car.

In the next scene with him, though, she does reject his advances. This scene is related thematically to those on either side of it—both involve Giovanni. In the previous sequence he is looking for Valentina but finds Resy. He tells her a little story and chats for a moment. It's not long though before he tires of her company as she has nothing to offer him—her relationship to others is entirely one of taking, not of giving. And so it is with Roberto. His long conversation with Lidia is shot from outside the car. As we don't hear what they say, we assume that it is not worth hearing. If part of the reason for Lidia's rejection of him lies in Roberto himself, what she actually says is 'I can't.' The suggestion of conscience links with the next sequence in which the first words are Valentina's 'I draw the line at home-wrecking.' The car ride itself is another of Antonioni's journeys. Lidia's progress away from Giovanni is halted physically when the car has to stop at a railroad crossing. The symbolism is taken even further by having them get out of the car before Roberto tries to kiss Lidia and she refuses. One can see what Antonioni is aiming at. It just seems a little ludicrous to make them get out of the car and stand in the pouring rain to help the imagery.

But the following scenes with Valentina show Antonioni at his best, aided enormously by Vitti's performance. In the character of Valentina there is greater self-awareness and sensitivity to others than we've seen before in Antonioni. Her order to the servant to bring more candles for her room (the electric light has failed) is symbolic of her part in the film.

Valentina is able to describe her own feelings with a clarity which was previously the sole prerogative of the director. 'Tonight I was feeling sad. Then as I played with you, it passed. Now it's coming back. It's like the sadness of a dog.' She wants to be as honest about her relationships with others. 'It seems to me that love limits a person. It's a bit of a fraud—creating emptiness around us.' We learn later in the scene that her honesty upsets other people, and that she's recently had an unhappy love affair.

Encouraged by the understanding he finds in her, Giovanni tries to explain his troubles: 'I believe now that I'm no longer capable of writing. I know what to write but not how to write.' Another parallel with Sandro in *L'Avventura:* Giovanni's personal life is reflected in his inability to work at his vocation. It's not his ideas and convictions that have been lost. He lacks the force necessary to create a work of art, to struggle at converting his ideas into a formal entity. For him it's a novel, for Sandro a building. The ideas are part of his make-up. They may change but they aren't lost. It's in the practical task of producing something concrete that Giovanni is vulnerable.

Valentina's reaction to his confession is typically both honest and deprecatory: 'You're weak, like me.' But why does he tell her this? She's just a girl who loves golf, etc. 'And beyond that there's nothing else you love?' Valentina replies sadly, 'Yes, everything.' She's encouraged by Giovanni's interest in her which one imagines is rather different from the attentions she's normally paid by men of her own class. After making him promise that he won't laugh at her, she plays him a tape recording of a short piece she has written herself.

A description of the 'useless sounds' she has to hear although she doesn't want to, it is a perceptive piece of writing. What it tells us about her (apart from her perceptiveness) is that she is troubled by the meaninglessness of most of the things she notices. She wishes to perceive only those things that have meaning. It's hardly being facetious to say that she'd like life to have the concentration of an Antonioni film.

When the recording is finished, Giovanni surprises Valentina by asking to hear it again.

She rewinds and turns on again. Silence. 'I erased it. Drivel!' Her destructiveness amazes Giovanni. Why did she do it? 'Because mine is not a compulsive vocation.' And when Giovanni says that she's wasting her intelligence, she replies with remarkable self-awareness, 'I'm not intelligent, just wide-awake. That's different. It's enough for me to observe things. I don't need to write about them.' As she talks she is playing with a wire toy which can be formed into various shapes, and holding it up to judge each one before going on to make another. Once Antonioni characters have plucked up the courage to talk honestly about themselves and really attempt to communicate, they are not to be stopped. When Giovanni tells her that they'll probably be seeing a lot of each other as her father has asked him to work there, Valentina goes right on with her own story. 'Last year I thought I was in love with a boy. But . . . I don't know . . . perhaps I'm not normal . . . perhaps I'll change, but each time I've tried to communicate with someone, love has disappeared.' The truth is painful and therefore has no place in a level of society whose perfect member is Momina of *Le Amiche.* 'Why are you going to work for my father—you don't need the money. . . . You need someone to help you get started again.' 'Not someone—you. Don't be afraid.' 'I'm not afraid.' He's about to kiss her when the lights come back on. 'You see, it's ridiculous,' says Valentina, seeing in the incident exactly the meaning Antonioni would give it.

Valentina and Giovanni confronted by Lidia and Roberto: two infidelities that didn't come off. Valentina takes Lidia into her room to dry. They start talking and discover that they like each other. Giovanni has been affected by his encounter with truthfulness in the shape of Valentina. So when Fanti, another millionaire, ends an anecdote about Hemingway with 'Still he's a man who knows his job. He's worth what he earns—millions of dollars and that's not to be rejected even by an intellectual,' Giovanni is able to say, 'It's difficult to decide what is, for an intellectual, to be rejected or kept.' He really becomes outraged at Roberto's contribution to the conversation—a facile quote from a book. 'Our age is antiphilosophical and weak,' etc. He is using this as a justification of his way of life, to shrug off personal responsibility: if our age is like that, why should he be any different? Giovanni's attack on Roberto is personal, as Roberto might, for all he knows, have made love to Lidia, and at the same time aimed at his way of life: 'I know that passage, the words of an author I admire. But quoted here they somehow disgust me . . . because the gentleman has spoken them with complacency, although they were written in desperation.'

Before this conversation, we have seen Lidia's hostility unable to survive the genuine kindness of Valentina. After Giovanni's little piece of self-assertion, they are confiding in each other, Valentina about her inability to fit in with others, Lidia about her desperation. She asks Valentina about her age—'Eighteen and many, many months.' 'You don't know what it is to be old and to feel that all those years no longer make sense. [At this point Giovanni comes in unnoticed.] I'd like to die tonight. I swear it. Then at least this agony would end and something new would begin.' 'Perhaps nothing.' With two flat words, Valentina stops Lidia's dramatization of her misery. As she and Giovanni are about to leave, Lidia says to Valentina, whom she now likes and pities, 'What I said before—it wasn't from any jealousy on my part. None at all. That's what's so wrong.' They exchange routine politenesses about seeing each other after the holidays. Valentina says, 'This year I shall come back later—much later.' Their farewells to Valentina are filled with tenderness, as she has shown them something that they did not have the

courage to admit before—the truth. In fact, she has said very little about them, but her remarks about herself are so honest in spite of her unhappiness, that with her they are forced to be honest about themselves. Giovanni strokes Valentina's cheek, Lidia kisses her. As the couple go out, Valentina says 'You've completely exhausted me, the two of you.' She kicks off a switch. In a beatiful image of her exhaustion, the light goes out obscuring her features and leaving her in silhouette against the dawn.

The couple walk out into the park, past Resy who has run out of interesting people and is sitting with a girl friend weeping profusely. In the cold but hopeful light of dawn, Giovanni tells Lidia of Gherardini's offer, which he says he will refuse. She in turn tells him of Tommaso's death and of what Tommaso has meant to her. 'He saw in me a power and intellect which I lack.' She talks about Tommaso's attempts to make her learn, how he talked only about her, how Giovanni had been something new in her life as he talked about himself. That was why she loved Giovanni, not Tommaso. Having broken the ice and started talking seriously to Giovanni she is able to tell him how she feels.

LIDIA: If I want to die, it's because I no longer love you. That's the reason for my despair. I would like to be old already, to have devoted my whole life to you. I don't want to exist any more because I can't love you. There. That's the thought that came to me in the night-club when you were so bored.

GIOVANNI: But if you tell me that, if you really want to die . . . that shows you still love me.

LIDIA: No, it's only pity.

GIOVANNI: I have given you nothing . . . I amount to nothing. I have wasted and I'm still wasting my life, like an idiot, taking without giving anything or giving too little in exchange. Perhaps I'm not worth much. If that's what you're going to say, you're right . . . it's strange

the feeling of them talking to one another but without being affected by the other's remarks. They are both talking into space, physically as well, because they're seated side by side looking out across the park rather than at each other. The scene is largely broken up into single-shots and two-shots of backs. What Lidia reads is a love-letter: it is a description of a man's feelings when he wakes up earlier than his mistress after their first night together. This reminder of their past is in a different spirit than the journey to their old meeting place in the suburbs. This is no attempt to rebuild what has been lost, only to show how things have changed. The letter ends:

'At that moment I realized how much I loved you, and my feelings were so intense that my eyes filled with tears because I thought that it must never end . . . that for me our whole life would be like waking up this morning—feeling you, not just beside me, but part of me, in a way that nothing or no one could destroy, except the tedium of habit which I feel as a threat hanging over us. And then you started to wake up gently. And smiling while you were still in your sleep, you kissed me, and I felt that I had nothing to fear—that we would always be as we were then—united by something stronger than time, stronger than habit.'

A pause, as Giovanni stares at Lidia, wondering why she has read this long letter to him (the quoted passage is only about a quarter of it). 'Who wrote it?' 'You did.' For me, at least, this does not really work as a scene. But whether or not one can believe that Giovanni would forget in this way, the intention is obvious—to show that time has changed a relationship that had seemed solid and permanent. The build-up of the letter, besides strengthening the emotional contrast that follows, calls to mind the reference to rhetoric in Antonioni's statement about the fragility of the emotions.

As the script puts it, 'Giovanni looks at her

that only today did I realize that what we give to others comes back to ourselves.

Lidia breaks in once to reminisce some more about Tommaso—that she would have let him make love to her out of boredom, but he never tried. Giovanni carries straight on from his previous thought. Although they are at last talking to each other, they are not having a conversation. Their trains of thought are hardly crossing. Lidia looks offscreen towards the musicians who are still playing.

LIDIA: What are they hoping for? That the day will be better if they play?

GIOVANNI: Lidia, let's give up this discussion. Let's try to build on something solid. I love you. . . . That's it. I'm sure that I've always loved you. What more do you want me to say? Let's go home.

We realize that Giovanni does not believe in what he's saying, that he's casting around for a way out from an embarrassing conversation. Lidia realizes that Giovanni has not fully understood the depth of the trouble. The reading of the letter is meant to be a way of bringing him to face the whole truth. It also crystallizes in silence, exhausted by the truth she has uncovered: their love no longer exists.' It is Lidia, who, like Claudia, has to make some sort of gesture. She puts her hand on Giovanni's. But this small gesture of pity is enough. Giovanni kisses her hand with almost the desperation of Tommaso at the beginning of the film. When he takes her in his arms, she tries to resist him, realizing that he wants to make love to her as an easy way of putting things right.

LIDIA: No . . . no . . . I don't love you any more . . . I don't love you any more. . . . And you . . . you don't love me.

GIOVANNI: Be quiet . . . be quiet.

LIDIA: Say it . . . say it.

GIOVANNI: No . . . I won't . . . I won't say it.

Lidia stops resisting. He pushes her back on to the ground. The script says (and I must take its word, as the British censor has had his mucky fingers on the film at this point)—'A sort of animal passion, a memory of what was, and what could be, grips them. And the caresses which Lidia and Giovanni exchange reveal this hope.' The camera tracks back diagonally from them, losing them and leaving only the golf

course in the cold, misty light of morning. The combination of bleakness and hope is that of *L'Avventura*.

Although the couple have escaped from the corrupt *milieu* of the Gherardini house, the conclusion is a compromise. Lidia only lets Giovanni make love to her because she hasn't the will to resist: she can't see any other hope for them. But the fact that Giovanni makes love to her indicates a desire on his part to maintain their relationship. Antonioni says it is 'the compromise which is found today in morality and even [!] in politics. The characters this time find themselves, but they have trouble in communicating because they have discovered that the truth is difficult, that it demands much courage and determination which is unattainable in their social environment.' In one way it is a more hopeful film than *L'Avventura* because it insists on the certainty of social as well as emotional change, and because this time the couple are helped by another character—Valentina. This is the first time in any Antonioni film that we are shown one person able to help others. In the earliest films, such attempts are automatically doomed. Here admittedly, she does not help them by a conscious action, but merely by her existence. Valentina herself is essentially a hopeful character—in spite of her unhappiness—as she is evidence that individuals can overcome the influences on them from a corrupt society.

La Notte has also progressed formally from *L'Avventura*. There is much heavier stressing of the general as well as the particular significance of each action.

As the method has become more rigorous, its snags have become more apparent. There is a tension between the genuineness of the behaviour which the audience can observe and the need to use it as an exposition of emotions. And in *La Notte* I start to feel that spontaneity has been sacrificed to exposition.

L'ECLISSE

L'Eclisse can be viewed as the third part of a loosely connected trilogy on personal relationships in postwar society. It is concerned with the same themes as its two predecessors, but it is as a partial reversal of them that it is the completion of the trilogy. Not that it is the opposite of them in the way that *L'Avventura* is the opposite of *Il Grido*. There the contrast was between the leading characters: a simple man who could not lose the memory of his past life and a sophisticated man who finds it only too easy to forget. In *L'Eclisse* the social level and the problems of the characters are very similar to those in *L'Avventura* and *La Notte*, but their choices are the reverse. It is this opposition which links the film to its predecessors—just as *Il Grido* and *L'Avventura* are connected by the contrast between them.

In style it is very much more fragmented and more detailed than either *La Notte* or *L'Avventura*, particularly in the first scene and the extraordinary ending. In the last 58 shots, about seven minutes, neither of the leading characters is seen. The fragmentation of the first scene is successful as an atmospheric device. It conveys that feeling of tiredness in which one takes in rather little except isolated details, a lack of contact with one's surroundings. Even in the long shots, our eyes are often drawn to a detail, like the small electric fan which pivots from side to side on its stand. Before either of the two characters start to talk, we realize from the evidence presented to us that it is early morning, that the couple have reached a crisis, that they have been talking all night and have nothing left to say to each other. We are aware of the time of day even before the girl draws back the curtains, letting in the light (a metaphor which has antecedents in *La Notte*) before

turning to face the man and say, 'Well, Riccardo?'

Riccardo (Francisco Rabal) is in his thirties, a well-to-do intellectual whose serious character is echoed in his chastely furnished apartment, and in the mainly abstract pictures which line the walls. The girl, Vittoria (Monica Vitti), is in her twenties and dressed well but simply in a plain black dress. Just now she is looking very tired but determined. For their first exchange the camera is oddly placed behind each of them in turn so that they are in line with it, and one is seen directly over the top of the other's head. The camera even tracks behind Vittoria in this position as she walks towards him. As he is sitting, these shots with her looking slightly down at him embody her determination compared to his abstraction which covers an unwillingness to come to grips with what is happening to them. Before this moment, although each has gazed at the other, the look has been avoided.

VITTORIA: Well, Riccardo?

RICCARDO: What is it?

VITTORIA: Everything that we've said tonight.

RICCARDO: Yes. Let's decide.

VITTORIA: It's already decided. I'm going.

Riccardo is struggling to keep alive a relationship that is already dead. One moment he bursts out desperately: 'What ought I to do. Go on, tell me what I can do and I'll do it.' The next he is miserable and almost begging for her pity: 'I wanted to make you happy.' To this last gambit she replies, 'When we met, I was twenty, and I was happy.' Riccardo goes out, she draws back some more curtains. In a gesture of frustration at the lack of resolution, she thumps the table with her fist. From the next room we hear the sound of Riccardo's electric razor.

We learn that Vittoria has been translating articles from the German for Riccardo. She is sorry that she can't go on with it, but knows someone who will do it instead. Riccardo, like Giovanni at the end of *La Notte*, will not admit that things have changed. But unlike Lidia, Vittoria does leave the man.

Riccardo has still not given up and this has a physical expression connected with the journey motif. He catches her in his car and then gets out and walks with her. He's always accompanied her home, so why not today? Just to break the silence he says, 'Vittoria, we've never

Still: Riccardo (Francisco Rabal) and Vittoria.

been out together so early in the morning.' He even suggests they have breakfast together. When they reach the block where she lives, her final words to him are rather apologetic: 'Well, goodbye . . . It was a terrible night for me too . . . I'm sorry.'

Her flat is also quite slick, but less expensively than Riccardo's. The furniture is modern. On the walls are record jackets and advertisements for art exhibitions. She looks out of her window at the trees outside stirring in the wind.

These seem to provide an image of instability as a comment on the breaking up of a relationship; the shot has an antecedent in *L'Avventura*. Claudia, standing alone in the car park at the end of that film before Sandro comes out to her, is seen against a background of willow trees shaken by the wind. The image makes other appearances later in *L'Eclisse*.

In the previous two films, a large part was played by money as a corrupting force. Sandro in *L'Avventura* has abandoned his vocation for the easy money he can make by estimating for a successful architect, Ettore. Gherardini in *La Notte* is a man whose only noticeable characteristic is his wealth. A measure of Lidia's desperation at the end of that film is her comment that Gherardini's offer of a job for Giovanni is a good opportunity. Whatever salvation the two couples achieve in these films it is partly due to their final (though not definitive) escapes from the world of Ettore and Gherardini.

This aspect appears more strongly in *L'Eclisse* where there is a direct conflict between feelings and money, without the complicating factor of artistic vocations. Piero (Alain Delon) is a stockbroker, the junior partner in a firm run by Ercoli (Louis Seignier). Vittoria meets him when she goes to the Rome Stock Exchange to look for her mother, needing someone to talk to after her break with Riccardo.

She arrives as a wave of buying and selling is building up. Delon is frantically buying up shares of one company as the price rises, so that he can sell them again at the top of the market and make a considerable profit. This time the money is presented as an end in itself rather than through its effects. Vittoria's mother is sitting in the area reserved for clients looking on attentively. She kisses her daughter and greets her with 'How come you're here?' Piero, who is the mother's broker, comes up to consult with her. As they discuss whether she is going to sell her shares, Vittoria watches with interest as if this is all strange to her. Piero advises mother to hang on to her shares until the price has risen further, to make some money. He turns to Vittoria and says 'You don't know me, but I know you. How are you?'

The business of the Stock Exchange is interrupted by a voice from a loudspeaker. It announces the death of one of the brokers in a motor accident and asks for a minute's silence in his memory. Vittoria and Piero are separated by a pillar. He leans round behind it to speak to her:

PIERO: We do a minute's silence like football players.

VITTORIA: Did you know him?

PIERO: Sure . . . but here, you know, in a minute millions change hands.

Suddenly at the end of the minute the noise starts again and everyone goes about his business as frantically as before.

The conversation when they get outside is not at all what Vittoria came for:

MOTHER: Do you want to know how much I made today?

VITTORIA: Mother, I've got to tell you something . . .

MOTHER: Tell me, darling . . .

But before Vittoria has a chance to confide in her, mother is haggling with a fruit seller about the price of some peaches. And when Vittoria remarks that it's not worth arguing about twenty lire, her mother's reply is a reminder that millions are made with lire. By this time Vittoria has lost all hope that her mother might be a possible source of comfort.

MOTHER: Listen . . . Where are you eating today? With Riccardo?

VITTORIA: Yes, with Riccardo.

The next section of the film is a series of diversions for Vittoria, perhaps as a way of forgetting herself. It starts with her entering her apartment at night and unwrapping a small parcel which turns out to contain a piece of rock with a fossil plant in it. She finds a hammer and nail and sets about hanging the fossil on the wall. But the noise brings in her next door neighbour, a young married woman called Anita, whose husband has been awakened.

As they talk, the telephone rings. Anita says a few words and turns to wave at a woman standing on a balcony higher up an adjacent block. This is Marta, to whom Anita is talking on the telephone. Marta's apartment is filled with all sorts of trophies which she and her husband collected in Kenya. She speaks with a slight foreign accent and uses occasional words in English and French. Vittoria is fascinated by the various exotica. She dresses up in native

Stills: Verona Airport; the minute's silence at the Stock exchange—Vittoria and Piero with her mother (Lilla Brignone) and Ercoli (Louis Seignier).

costume and blacks her face. Completely taken up with the spirit of pantomime, she does a little dance with a spear. The sequence connects with the business of the wigs in *L'Avventura*. Even in disguise Vittoria keeps her personality. But the hostess gets fed up with the game and says 'That's enough' in English. Vittoria stops, looking a little ashamed at her performance. Marta talks about life in Kenya. It's evident that she's very much a colonialist at heart. Everyone has revolvers there, because there are only 60,000 whites against 6 million Negroes.

Riccardo has not quite given up. Vittoria is lying in bed when he appears in the road outside her apartment, yelling her name and throwing pebbles at her window. Vittoria dresses hastily and telephones a friend. 'Franco . . . it's Vittoria . . . don't joke . . . it's serious . . . I've left Riccardo . . . it's a difficult moment for him . . . don't leave him alone.' The man's voice on

the telephone says 'You're alone too.'

The central part of the film has been cut very heavily in editing: whole scenes have been removed, either by Antonioni or by the Hakim brothers who produced the film and gave him a lot of trouble, as they did Losey, whose *Eva* they also produced. However, Antonioni did cut a lot out of *L'Avventura* in editing (mainly scenes illustrating Sandro's artistic crisis, which were probably too didactic in nature for the director's taste), and the missing scenes which are printed in John Francis Lane's book in the Cappelli series (by far the best presented of the Antonioni scripts) do seem less than essential. The first is between Vittoria and her mother who comes visiting when she hears from Riccardo that the affair is over. She is reproving although she didn't really like Riccardo who was a socialist.

Vittoria's air trip to Verona has also been cut, omitting conversations with the pilot who is Anita's husband, as they pass near a storm which scares Vittoria. Originally their arrival in Verona was an accident caused by a fault in their radio compass. In the final version all is calm. The sequence is restricted to shots of Vittoria with Anita and others from her point of view—the trailing edge of the wing and landscape behind it, and the backs of the pilots. 'Let's go through that cloud,' cries Vittoria happily. The choice of camera positions invites us to share in her enjoyment of flying, for this is the only time in the film that we see Vittoria free from emotional troubles. The journey away from Rome is also a journey away from her troubles.

The mood of the sequence at Verona Airport is of warmth and well-being induced by the surroundings, not by other people, as part of her happiness seems to stem from the fact that life is not complicated by relationships with others. Anita and her husband have left her

alone. She is just enjoying the sun and watching the planes landing and taking off. She wanders up to the airport café, looks at a couple of negroes sitting at a table, ignores an American at the bar when he says hello to her, and sits down outside. This is the third reference in the film to colour, but they do not seem to be tied together at all. Vittoria is an outsider who is just observing the things around her, as she did before in the Stock Exchange. Lidia in *La Notte*, as she walks around Milan and its outskirts, is also isolated from the people she sees, which deepens her desperation as it extends her feeling of estrangement from her husband. Vittoria's isolation, on the other hand, comes as a relief from the business of coping with other people—throughout the film she is avoiding or severing relationships rather than trying to build them. She shies away from rela-

tionships which involve interdependence.

Back to the Stock Exchange. Piero is brandishing a minute portable electric fan. Later we see it in the hands of another broker. During the very long sequence in the Stock Exchange, we watch apprehension build up into panic during a recession in the market. As prices fall, and more and more brokers are trying to sell, the apparent chaos which we saw before during Piero's buying spree is even greater. Everyone is running to and from the telephones. Piero rushes into a box, picks up the receiver and tells the operator that she's a pig if she doesn't get him Florence immediately. A couple of hours later, the Stock Exchange is packed and news is beginning to come in of similar recessions abroad: Wall Street is weak, and they're selling in Frankfurt. When Vittoria arrives, gloom is general, and her mother is acting as if she had lost everything. She bewails her loss as if it were her nearest and dearest that had gone—and in a way it is. She blames the socialists, who are undermining everything.

Vittoria is fed up with her mother's stupidity, but is nevertheless curious to know whether there is any foundation for her misery.

VITTORIA: Is what happened really serious?
PIERO: With money, everything rights itself . . . for some it's a disaster . . . a complete disaster.
VITTORIA: And for my mother?
PIERO: For your mother it shouldn't be a drama . . . she's lost about ten million lire.

He points out a man who has lost two or three hundred million. Vittoria is fascinated by this man who has lost so much money at one time, and she follows him. He buys some pills and goes into a café for a drink to wash them down. He scribbles something on a slip of paper. When he has gone, Vittoria picks it up. He has drawn some placid little flowers. Piero is not very interested in this: he shrugs his shoulders as if to say 'How silly!' and starts dialling a number on the café's telephone. 'You never stop,' Vittoria remarks. Piero looks baffled: 'Why should I stop?' Vittoria's curiosity about the Stock Exchange is not yet satisfied. 'Where do all those millions they lost in the Stock Exchange end up?' 'Nowhere.' Piero's answers to her questions leave her just as puzzled. The more they talk and get to know each other, the less common ground they can find for communication, let alone agreement.

In the remaining scenes, we learn more about them at the same time as they get to know each other—up to this point we know very little about Vittoria's life and nothing about Piero's except that he is a broker. The first stage is a visit to Vittoria's mother who's 'not the flower-drawing type.' They arrive at her apartment before her. Compared to Vittoria's it is run-down—the wallpaper bears the shadows left by pictures which have been taken down. On a sideboard are a large number of photographs. They show a couple, her mother and father, on their wedding day, and later. We see the pictures in close-up, and it's obvious that her parents were very poor. Vittoria cannot understand why her mother keeps them; now she's secure her husband's memory doesn't matter to her.

VITTORIA: That's what my mother's afraid off: poverty.

PIERO: Everyone's afraid of that.

VITTORIA: I don't think we are. Just as I don't think about becoming rich.

In her bedroom she draws in the dust on the furniture, and then lies down on the bed, which is much too short for her. Piero sits beside her. When he bends over to kiss her, she avoids him, and gets up; nothing else can happen as her mother then arrives home.

In the office of the broker Ercoli clients are gathering to find out the worst and to blame him and Piero. Eventually Piero gets so angry that he bawls out one little man. 'When you came to me you had only 200,000 lire . . . do you remember that? In two years I made you seven or eight million . . . then I told you to stop and you wouldn't . . . you got greedy . . . because of that you lost a few million.' In spite of the man's feeble protestations at the onslaught, Piero tells him that it's his fault, that he should try getting his money back some place else. He terminates the meeting with a vehement 'You make me sick!' The lusting for money which Piero despises in his clients, including Vittoria's mother, is only a less sophisticated version of his work—it is not really the greed itself that bothers him.

Before we see Piero and Vittoria together again, we are shown the way he treats his other girl friends. He leaves the office to go down to the '*bestiola*' who is waiting for him. She turns out to be an attractive and well-dressed girl, who is perhaps a little plump and, one would guess, not very bright. She has obviously been waiting some time. In the first shot of her we

see her through the grille which protects the window display of the jeweller's shop outside which she is waiting. She is annoyed at the start and when he asks her why she has dyed her hair, she takes offence. Piero would probably not be too keen at the best of times: someone to sleep with occasionally, but no more. And tonight he is not particularly interested:

GIRL: Let's go.

PIERO: Where do you want to go?

GIRL: And what are we going to do?

PIERO: You're right. You go and I'll stay here.

When she has gone, he strolls along the pavement, whistling to himself. On a sudden impulse he leaps into his Alfa-Romeo which is parked in the street and drives off very fast. Dissolve to the road outside Vittoria's apartment as Piero drives past. Vittoria is sitting by the window typing. A drunk who is tottering past calls up to her 'Ciao cara.' She smiles 'Ciao, but who are you?' The drunk lurches off just as Piero comes into view.

PIERO: Good evening.

VITTORIA: 'Evening.

PIERO: What are you typing?

VITTORIA: I'm translating some material from the Spanish.

PIERO: How does one say 'Can I come up?' in Spanish?

VITTORIA: One says 'Not a chance.' Nasty language, eh, Spanish.

PIERO: I don't see why we should lose time like this.

VITTORIA: Me neither.

We see that they have quickly come to like each other, which is hardly surprising as they are both young and attractive. Before the conversation has time to progress further, Piero's car comes racing down the road with the drunk at the wheel. Vittoria does not know where there is a police station and lets Piero in to telephone.

The next morning Piero is watching his car

being fished out of the artificial lake made for the Olympic boating events. Vittoria also turns up out of curiosity. She is horrified to learn that the car contains a corpse, more so when she discovers that it is the friendly drunk of the night before. Piero's worries are rather different.

PIERO: They should be hauling it out of the water very slowly. The body will be nothing but dents.

VITTORIA: You're only thinking about the body.

PIERO: I'm also thinking about the engine . . . it'll take at least a week to repair.

He decides to sell the car. As they walk away, Vittoria asks him if she's making him waste time. He answers tactlessly that she isn't and anyway he had to come. Vittoria laughs but he is embarrassed. Before he can explain, Vittoria says 'On the other hand I came to see you. Am I stupid?' Now Piero smiles, as he finds this flattering. Vittoria turns to him and suddenly becomes serious. The scene has a peculiarly uneasy feeling caused by a sort of dislocation between the words and the reactions. Once again we are shown that they like each other a lot, but aren't able to communicate. There is a tension between their shared physical enjoyment and the differences that come out in conversation, even over little things.

A little piece of shared fun: they find a balloon tied to a deserted baby-carriage outside the block where Marta lives. Vittoria calls up to her to get her rifle. They free the balloon, and Marta bursts it as it floats past her balcony. They are happy together in this way. He does a little caper as they walk along and then they bow to each other. They come to a pedestrian crossing. 'When we get to the other side,' he says, 'I'll kiss you.' But she doesn't let him, although he tries twice. The background is of leafy branches rustling in the wind—the second

Stills: Vittoria and Piero.

appearance of that motif. 'I'm going,' she says, and walks away before he can say anything. She seems already to sense the differences between them. One can see other reasons for not letting him kiss her in mother's apartment, when, after all, they were alone together for the first time.

That night she telephones him but does not reply when she hears his voice. He gets more and more annoyed, shouting 'Pronto! . . . Pronto! . . . Pronto!' before slamming down the receiver. Next afternoon, though, she is waiting for him at the spot where she left him the previous day. She has to wait for some time before he shows up. The place is a street corner from which can be seen one of the pylons supporting the floodlights for the Olympic Stadium. On the corner is a building site with its scaffolding screened from view by straw matting. Beside it are heaps of airbricks and a water barrel. A very typical Antonioni location.

Piero's apartment is large and old-fashioned, probably typical of a wealthy bourgeois family: rich dark wallpapers, one or two large, rather sentimental paintings, oval framed photographs, and a bronze statuette of a knight in armour—'What's that?' 'It's always been there.' Vittoria, who is used to something a little more chic and modern, is surprised that a young man should have such a large and gloomy place.

VITTORIA: You live here?

PIERO: Not always. I was born here. . . . Do you want something to drink?

VITTORIA: No. When you're not staying here, where do you live?

Piero is embarrassed.

PIERO: Well . . . I have another apartment, a smaller one.

VITTORIA: A love nest. Why didn't you take me there?

PIERO: Do you want a chocolate?

He is baffled by this girl who is happy to talk frankly about the subjects which, one imagines, his other girl friends would avoid. When he hands her a box of chocolates, she tells him not to treat her like a visitor. She asks him what he did the previous evening. He had dinner with a millionaire. 'Or with a call girl?' 'And what time do I have to go with call girls,' he says, and then adds jokingly 'The call girl is me.' He asks Vittoria what she did. 'So many questions. One doesn't need to know someone to love them. . . . But then . . . one doesn't need to be loved.' She was with friends last night. He wouldn't know them as they're not on the Stock Exchange. She has realized that he leads a very limited life. He tries to explain the fascination of the stock market, but can only say that when you get caught up in it, it becomes enthralling.

Again there is the contrast between the conversation and the accord in the love scenes. Their first kiss is through the glass of a bookcase door: this may seem corny, and the sort of thing one remembers seeing before somewhere, but in its context it seems right, as well as foreshadowing the playfulness of the final love scene. As they kiss a second time, passionately —without the glass—the shoulder of Vittoria's dress is torn apart. She goes off into his bedroom. She takes off her necklace and is beginning to undress, when the sound of a church clock striking the hour makes her pause for a moment. She looks around the room, and seems to be intimidated by the gloomy luxury and the family portraits. Indeed the only relief from the mood of the room is the light from the window. Vittoria goes over and looks out. A group of people come out of the church. A soldier is leaning against a wall eating an ice-cream. We hear Piero's voice outside, asking if he can come in. She tells him that he can't, but begins to open the door just as he comes in through another door. After a beautifully contrived piece of business—a little game with their hands —they begin to make love passionately.

Cut to a pair of male feet with the almost

conical shape of the indoor Olympic cycling track in the background. The sharp drop in temperature marks a contrast in mood, for this is to be another dialogue scene. The feet are Piero's. He and Vittoria are lying on a grassy bank.

PIERO: Then you won't marry me?

VITTORIA: I don't have any nostalgia for marriage.

PIERO: Where does nostalgia come into it. You've never been married.

Still: the final embrace.

VITTORIA: No, I didn't mean that.

The scene ends on a note of complete incomprehension: Piero cannot understand why Vittoria is unwilling to enter into any permanent relationship.

Final scene of physical happiness. Piero and Vittoria are lying on a couch in Ercoli's office. It is too narrow for both of them—'There's always one arm too many.' The love scene is all laughter. Again there is the kiss through glass and a lot of happy romping on the floor. The doorbell rings. They both look up. Piero doesn't answer it although it rings two or three times, but Vittoria looks serious because she's begin-

ning to feel embarrassed. 'It's late,' she says, 'for you not for me.' They straighten their clothes and go out into the hall. Their final embrace is very serious.

PIERO: I'll see you tomorrow?

Vittoria nods.

PIERO: I'll see you tomorrow and the day after.

VITTORIA: . . . and the next day and the one after that . . .

PIERO: . . . and the one after . . .

VITTORIA: . . . and tonight.

PIERO: At eight. Usual place.

They exchange a final look as she goes out. She walks down the stairs. The stairwell is boarded up, which somehow seems threatening. He goes back into the office and replaces the receivers of the four telephones which he had taken off while she was there. Her descent, moving away from him is intercut with shots of him as the telephones all begin to ring and he does nothing about them. She emerges into the street. We see her standing outside the jeweller's shop where Piero's cast-off *bestiola* waited for him. Then a shot of her seen through the grille, just like the other girl, from which Antonioni tilts away to the trees on the other side of the road. Cut to the trees without the grille in the foreground. Pan back to her as she turns and looks at the door of the offices, and walks out of frame. The traffic noises stop.

That is the last we see of either of the leading characters. There are still 58 shots and about seven minutes to go before the end title. The sequence is a montage of shots of the corner where Piero and Vittoria met, and the area around it, passing from late afternoon to night. Originally this was not to be a montage sequence and was preceded by a scene in which Vittoria meets Riccardo in the street. They greet each other as acquaintances, but nothing more, and go their separate ways.

The no-characters montage sequence is not done in the dialectical manner of Resnais;

L'Eclisse is not *Rome mon amour*.

The main components of the sequence are shots of things and people that we have seen before when Piero and Vittoria were meeting. A nurse wheeling a carriage. The matting which cover the building works on the corner. A horse and carriage for trotting races. The water barrel into which Vittoria threw a twig while she was waiting for Piero. The pylon with the floodlights for the stadium.

The second series of shots which appear during the sequence mark the time of day but are also in themselves worrying or sinister. Two buses pass. The second one turns the corner so that the wheel comes very close to the camera. A man gets out reading a paper; the headline on the front page is THE ATOMIC RACE. People are going home. The fountain which has been playing in the EUR gardens is turned off at dusk. The street lights go on. Another bus passes.

There is a third stream of shots in the sequence which are atmospheric or symbolic. Again we see trees in the wind. The bark on a tree trunk with ants crawling on it. Water trickling away out of the bottom of the water barrel; the camera tracks to follow the course of the water until it reaches a culvert. Three shots of the jagged outline of a building with balconies which jut out, seen almost in silhouette. The noise of a jet plane (recalling *La Notte*). The last shot is almost despairingly cold and abstract: a huge close-up of a street lamp, surrounded by a halo of light.

Twice in the course of the last seven minutes we are reminded of the leading characters, both times as double takes. The camera tracks across the road behind a man who could be Piero or Riccardo but turns out not to be. A blonde girl waits for someone. We hope that it is Vittoria, but again we are disappointed. The disappointment involves the audience more closely in the failure of Piero and Vittoria to keep their date.

Our most recent memory of them is as attractive and charming young people. We are sorry that they are breaking·up.

The feeling of the final sequence, though, is much stronger than this. At a first viewing I was quite terrified by the ending of *L'Eclisse*, much more than by most things which are calculated to terrify. (By the second viewing, some of the emotional effect had already evaporated: perhaps part of it was a feeling of apprehension at what might have been about to happen.) I think this comes from the coldness which builds up during the sequence as night falls. The feeling is one of solitude—even the shots of people are of people alone. Antonioni said that at the end of *L'Avventura* the protagonists had arrived at a mutual sense of pity. 'What else is left if we do not at least succeed in achieving this?' Piero and Vittoria have failed to establish a relationship. Although they are fond of each other and physically attracted, their outlooks on life are so different that they cannot find any real understanding. And what is left? Solitude.

The other thing that makes this conclusion frightening is its lack of specificity. The shots could be of the evening after their last meeting in Ercoli's office, when they fail to turn up for their date, but it could equally be any other evening. We are invited to generalize, to conclude with Antonioni that solitude is man's usual state. Although the invitation has never been so clear as in the conclusion of *L'Eclisse*, we are expected to do so in all three films, to relate the actions not just to the characters themselves, but to put them in their social, political and temporal context. All the small external references in the films point the way to this—diverse examples: unemployment, a rock number, a revolutionary design of motor yacht (*L'Avventura*), socialism, the replanning of cities, industrial relations (*La Notte*), the Twist, the colour problem, the bomb (*L'Eclisse*). Very closely tied to the time at which they were made, the films are in no way didactic, that is, they do not set out to make a comment, but only to present the director's view of the world.

This view is consistent throughout the three pictures. The appearance of *L'Eclisse* would seem to make superfluous discussions of whether the ending of *La Notte* is more or less optimistic than the ending of *L'Avventura*, and indeed whether either is optimistic at all. We see from the contrasting example of Piero and Vittoria that although it is possible to generalize from the problems which face the characters in all the films, the resolutions are specific and depend on the individual psychology of each of the couples. Finally the value of Antonioni lies less in the generalities than in the observation and the manner of presenting behaviour. In the three films, his triumph which is total only in *L'Avventura* and is marred by a number of moments in *La Notte*, is the maintenance of spontaneity in the face of the most intricate calculation in the *mise-en-scène*.

The form of the 'trilogy' comes from the parallel between the first two films, particularly in their endings which are countered by *L'Eclisse*. The first two end at dawn with a renewal of a relationship which had been partly destroyed during the previous night. *L'Eclisse* starts at dawn with the breaking of a relationship: Vittoria leaves Riccardo's apartment alone, whereas the other couples escape together from the place where they have spent the night. The dawn symbolizes self-knowledge and a fresh beginning. At the end of *L'Eclisse*, Piero remains in Ercoli's office which is an image of capitalism, like the hotel in *L'Avventura* and Gherardini's house in *La Notte*. Vittoria leaves alone again. Consistent with the symbolism of the previous films, *L'Eclisse* ends with the coming of night. The last sequence of Antonioni's trilogy of change centres on the image of progress which was already to be seen in the opening sequence of its first film: a building site.

COLOUR FILMS

Whatever one thinks of Antonioni as an artist, no one who cares about the artist's role in contemporary civilisation can deny his importance as a case. His films have demonstrated again and again, beyond any reasonable doubt, that he possesses to a high degree on the one hand the intelligence and sensibility, on the other the ambition, of the major artist.

I shall consider in detail *Il Deserto Rosso* and *Blow Up*; but in order to establish my view of Antonioni's later work, to provide the perspective within which I want to examine these two films, I find it necessary, given the organic nature of his development, to go back to *L'Avventura*. Antonioni at that time was already used to working in (by film-making standards) conditions of reasonable creative freedom. The swift and widespread international success, both critical and commercial, of *L'Avventura* decisively established his right to freedom and must have enormously increased his confidence: the style, themes and tone of *L'Avventura* are developed uncompromisingly through the subsequent work up to and including *Il Deserto Rosso*.

L'Avventura is a great film; yet the doubts one always had about it have been amply confirmed by its successors. As a psychological narrative it is unassailable, the characters and their relationships examined and developed with masterly insight and subtlety. Yet a work of *L'Avventura*'s manifest pretensions inevitably offers itself as something more than that. Confronted with an artist as serious, ambitious, and intelligent as Antonioni, one must see his characters not merely as people-in-a-story, but as representative figures pointing outwards to wider issues. If this is granted, then certain reservations about the film immediately present themselves: reservations centred upon the character of Sandro. Representative Sandro is, fairly enough; but representative of modern creative life at such a low level as seriously to limit (rather than undermine) the film's validity as an exploration of the creative possibilities in modern life—in work and in relationships. Sandro is from the outset such a feeble specimen, putting up no real struggle anywhere against his weaknesses, his readiness to succumb to temptations, that the overall significance of the film becomes not so much tragic as defeatist. The character is too slight to sustain the weight of generalisation the film compels one to impose on him. Sandro's representative significance is also weakened by the fact that his defeat does not seem explainable in the terms suggested by the film, but only in terms of undefined and unacknowledged personal neurosis. One must beware of the critical impertinence of telling a director what he ought to make films about, but this does not absolve the critic from the responsibility of standing back from the work to assess the value and validity of what it actually does. One conclusion seems inescapable: by making Sandro's case so hopeless from the start, Antonioni simplifies to the point of evasion the central problems of creativity in contemporary society. Why did he choose as protagonist an artist so manifestly inferior to himself? Doesn't Sandro's inbuilt defeat make the whole film much easier than it would have been with a more active, positive central figure? And isn't the tendency to languor and mannerism inherent in Antonioni's style (but in *L'Avventura* still reasonably under control) intimately connected with choosing this type of protagonist? Defeatism is by definition self-indulgent, and an artist can scarcely build on a more unsound basis.

Antonioni's achievement appears in a more favourable light if one compares it with that of a director whose career, superficially so different, exhibits such striking parallels. It is evident enough now—it should, perhaps, have been evident all along—that Losey is intrinsically the inferior artist. Even the least acceptable of Antonioni's mature films is artistically more coherent than *The Servant*, with its disturbing discrepancy between intellectual concept and emotional effect—the impression one takes from it that what really involved its director emotionally had little to do with the imposed allegory, the willed gesturings towards a larger social significance. The emotional world of Losey's later films is more perniciously constricting and degrading than that of Antonioni, who at least conveys to the spectator an aesthetic beauty and a certain compassion (for what they are worth): beside *The Servant*, *L'Eclisse* looks positively open and generous.

Asked who was the greatest French poet, André Gide replied, *Victor Hugo, hélas!* One could reply to the question, which of Antonioni's and Losey's films are their greatest, in the same spirit: respectively, *L'Avventura* and *Eve, hélas*. The tendencies that vitiate most of their subsequent work—Antonioni's self-indulgent defeatism, the morbid preoccupation with systematic degradation and destruction that seems to me to characterize Losey's films—are already powerful presences, but they are just adequately counterbalanced by healthier pulls to be held in check. One may prefer *Le Amiche* or *Blow Up* (just as one may prefer *Time Without Pity* or *The Damned* to *Eve*), but it is impossible not to see *L'Avventura* as a larger work and a more complete expression of its director than anything Antonioni had made before it, and less enervating than the other larger works that were to follow.

The borderline separating a near-masterpiece from an artistic disaster can be at times very narrow and difficult to define. Such a borderline separates *L'Avventura* from *La Notte*. They seem at first sight to be so alike; and indeed the resemblance isn't deceptive or misleading. But the earlier film seems to me decisively distinguished from the later by the presence in it of an alive sense of exploration. Though all Antonioni's defeatist tendencies are strongly present, and work consistently against its exploratory vitality, it is a much more 'open' film than *La Notte*. Here Sandro turns up again. only rather more so; indeed, everything in *La Notte* is rather more so. While visiting a friend in hospital he (now called Giovanni) gets himself seduced by a nymphomaniac in the psychiatric ward, and discovered by his wife. So we know at the outset where we are: it sets the tone for the whole film. Giovanni has no moral fibre whatever: by which I mean not only that he lacks all sense of propriety, but that he lacks any vital instinctual awareness of other people. On the other hand, he isn't letting fly at life in some abandoned existential fling. He is just very feeble, almost pathologically so: his fibres have gone soft, he is a victim of Degeneration of the Tissues, nervous, mental, moral, emotional, instinctual. So we have what feels like hours of Jeanne Moreau wandering the streets looking glum, as only Mlle Moreau knows how.

About halfway through this seemingly interminable night (Antonioni deserves all praise for the consummate artistry with which he communicates the characters' sense of tedium to the spectator), our director seems to have a moment of real self-awareness—as opposed to self-*consciousness*, which he is never without—in which he realises that the totally negative and defeatist attitude in which the film has so far luxuriated might be proving a bit of a drag. So he hastily introduces a Positive Value, in the shape of Miss Monica Vitti being Spontaneous. Miss Vitti's spontaneity in this film is a bit daunting: it looks so *willed*. Also, it exists in a vacuum, unsupported and unaccounted for. As the socialite daughter of a wealthy industrialist, the character hardly exists; as a Positive Value she is about as real, and about as much practical use, as Mr Bergman's mediaeval jesters.

As content dwindles and shrivels, or becomes increasingly a matter of self-indulgence and easily accepted defeat as the surest way of not having to face problems, so, inevitably, Aestheticism and Style become more and more obtrusive, in *La Notte* and *L'Eclisse* and still, in different forms, in *Il Deserto Rosso*. The mannerisms evolved in *L'Avventura* become maddening personal clichés, stock reactions, almost gross. A point is reached where one feels one must scream the next time a head slides into a hitherto 'blank' image from the side of the screen. *La Notte* and *L'Eclisse* are not so much great films as great monstrous perversions of the creative intelligence. When you begin to see them as such they become quite interesting and you can keep awake; as Great Works of Art they are almost entirely soporific. The sense of exploration has gone; everything is conscious and deliberate, everything is known.

These films seem to me dangerously susceptible to the somewhat facile ridicule to which I have surrendered: as, let us say, Bergman's *Winter Light* and *The Silence* are not. People *do* scoff at *The Silence* but the film is not harmed by it: rather, the laughter rebounds, because the ridicule is so obviously defensive. Awareness of absurdity is never far below the surface of Bergman's film and erupts repeatedly during it (especially through the use of the dwarfs); its tone of tragic intensity is never far removed from macabre farce, and knows it. *La Notte* and *L'Eclisse*, on the other hand, have the air of being entirely unaware that anyone might find them absurd. There is nothing complacent about the expression of anguish in the Bergman films; his ruthless stripping down of style contrasts sharply with the proliferation of mannerisms in Antonioni. In describing my ridicule as somewhat facile, I don't mean that I didn't mean it: simply that it soon becomes impossible (if one allows oneself to think and feel about the films freely) to mean *only* that. The films are harmed by ridicule; they are by no means annihilated. They seem to me very deeply flawed, constituting a betrayal of much of what is essential in art. The function of art is clearly very complex, capable of many complementary or semi-contradictory definitions. But a part of that function, it seems to me, must be to make the recipient in some sense more *alive*—not necessarily happy (though I think some form of joy is stimulated by successful art, even the most pessimistic or desperate), but alert, responsive, *active*. The whole movement of *La Notte* and *L'Eclisse* seems to work in the opposite direction, so that they become a sort of depressive aesthetic drug. At the same time one can hardly deny that the films contain much that is central to contemporary emotional experience, or that they show a great deal of insight in the details of psychological observation This limited artistic excellence and relevance, combined with their perfection of expression and Antonioni's marvellous control of rhythm (hence, if one is willing to succumb, of spectator response), make them the ideal medium for the self-indulgence of disillusioned intellectuals. Even their desolation is strangely comforting, because it is so little disturbed by any activeness of protest, and so beautifully expressed. There are many ways of seeking refuge from the complexities, confusions and anxieties of a profoundly disturbing age; Antonioni's retreat into a fundamentally complacent despair is a particularly subtle and insidious one, because it gives the impression all the time of uncompromisingly confronting them.

There is a striking consistency in the relationships depicted in Antonioni's films, from *L'Avventura*, through *La Notte* and *L'Eclisse* to *Il Deserto Rosso*, the common factor being the inadequacy of the men to satisfy the women. The woman's frustrations are the emotional core of all four films (in three out of the four, the frustrations are Miss Vitti's). There is a significant shift, almost exactly halfway through this tetralogy, in the *nature* of the men's inadequacy. Sandro and Giovanni are artists: men, that is to say, who by reasons of their vocation might be expected to show an awareness of the perspective of existence rooted in a coherent, not necessarily consciously defined, metaphysic, characterized by sensitivity and a generous emotional understanding. They have failed in their vocation as artists to the extent to which they fail to meet such demands, and they fail lamentably. Both are traitors to art, and to

themselves: to their creative instincts, which in effect *are* their selves. Both have sold out to the commercial-materialist world. Hence they are quite incapable of meeting the demands made on them by women: unable to look themselves in the eye, how can they possibly meet the eyes of their women? The inadequacy of Piero in *L'Eclisse* and Ugo in *Il Deserto Rosso* is quite other: they look their women in the eye readily enough, and are scarcely aware of being inadequate. Piero is a man of finance, Ugo a man of science. Both are thoroughly adapted to life in an exclusively materialistic universe. The finer sensibilities of Sandro and Giovanni are incurably corrupted; those of Piero and Ugo are quite simply dead, they have ceased to exist. Riccardo in *L'Eclisse* provides the bridge from the exploration of the one to the exploration of the other: the opening ten minutes of the film are a succinct recapitulation of the essence of *L'Avventura* and *La Notte*. After that, a new direction is taken. Corrado in *Il Deserto Rosso* is interesting in being the only male character in any of these films to combine elements of both types. Really, poor Giuliana gets the worst of both worlds—the disabling uncertainties of the one and the insensitivity of the other. Thomas in *Blow Up* is even more interesting because as a photographer he is a neat amalgam of artist and scientist—neither one nor the other, but a little bit of both; he begins in the Piero-Ugo line of limited and insulated self-sufficiency and is systematically broken down (or opened up?) as the film progresses.

The films treat centrally the basic problem of the relationship between men and women in our century. (It is perhaps the rather marginal treatment of it in *Blow Up* that makes one feel that that film, however much one may prefer it to the others, is comparatively lightweight, as if Antonioni were there side-stepping what has been consistently the emotional centre of his work.) The proposition that by nature man is the adventurer, woman the conservator and stabiliser,no longer meets with universal acceptance, yet has much to be said for it in strictly biological and practical terms, leaving aside the more intangible and arguable issues of emotional and spiritual being. Some such proposition seems basic to Antonioni's work, with its analysis of modern man's betrayal of himself, hence of woman. As society 'progresses', man's adventuring becomes more and more exclusively scientific-technological. The artist is left either to corrupt himself by surrendering to commercial success or in a state of impotent uncertainty, turned in upon himself and needing continual reassurance from outside to sustain his ego. The scientist finds the centre of his being in an education and a life that do not encourage that finer awareness of human feeling that one supposes the arts to develop. Hence the frustrations of Antonioni's women, from Claudia (*L'Avventura*) to Giuliana (*Il Deserto Rosso*).

Still: Monica Vitti as Giuliana in Il Deserto Rosso.

IL DESERTO ROSSO

In essential characteristics as in theme, *Il Deserto Rosso* belongs with its three immediate predecessors, in some respects carrying their tendencies to new extremes. Here for the first time the protagonist is overtly presented as neurotic, and therefore *explicitly* incapable of fulfilling her inner needs. At the same time, certain aspects of the film mark a new phase in Antonioni's development. In obvious ways he was breaking new ground, working in a milieu remote from the intellectual-socialite world of the preceding films, and shooting for the first time in colour. These factors may be partly responsible for the comparatively open and exploratory nature of *Il Deserto Rosso*.

One of the keys to the film is the only scene from which Giuliana is entirely absent: the scene where Corrado (Richard Harris) talks to the workers about conditions in Patagonia. He answers their questions with increasing detachment, turning to indifference. His eye rests first on an electric wire-end sticking out of a wall, on the necks of empty bottles, on a pile of baskets, then on an apparently arbitrary blue line that climbs a wall and turns off to one side; the practical reality of objects drains away, and the world becomes a strange confusion of abstract shapes. We understand that Corrado's vitality and decisiveness are being paralysed by a growing sense that the whole enterprise, perhaps all human endeavour, is futile. His experience is conveyed partly with soft-focus shots of workers and backgrounds, which are used far more extensively elsewhere to convey Giuliana's sense of isolation from her surroundings—her alienation. The scene provides a link between them that is confirmed later when Corrado says, about her illness, 'We all suffer from it a bit. Some more, some less. We're all searching for

a cure.' We saw, from the start of their relationship, that Corrado was attracted to her precisely because of her neurotic condition, and that condition has gradually communicated itself to him, finding fertile soil in his own doubts about himself and his vocation in which to develop. His abstracted following of the blue line recalls the conversation between him and Giuliana on the rig at sea (a setting that evokes the sense of instability and impermanence that is central to the characters' condition), during which Antonioni uses the unpredictable and seemingly arbitrary bendings of pipes to express their shared feeling of strangeness. The relationship is later to culminate in the scene where Cerrado makes love to Giuliana because she is on the verge of insanity.

Like so much else in the film, his behaviour here is extremely ambiguous. Antonioni (in the interview published in *Movie 12*) sees him merely as 'taking advantage of her and of her state of mind' ('. . . it is her own world which betrays her . . .'); but it is at least as valid (and the two views, though seemingly contradictory, are not incompatible) to see his actions as motivated by an extreme protective tenderness which is as much concern for his own vulnerability as for hers. He is drawn to her because she expresses in an extreme form his own innermost tendencies; she represents for him also the *temptation* of defeat, as a means of evading the need to struggle. Contrary to general opinion, I think Richard Harris is very well used in the film: the zombie-like face and movements convey very exactly the character's unacknowledged spiritual bewilderment, hinted at in a number of small but betraying gestures and flickers of expression. As he and Ugo watch the terrifying release of steam in the factory-yard, he puts his hands over his ears while the other stands calm and unmoved, hands in pockets. His complex attitude to Giuliana during the first scene in her 'shop'—hesitant, suspended between fear and attraction—is very revealing. Corrado's function in the film, then, is roughly analogous to that of Marion Crane in *Psycho*: he represents a reflection, within a recognisable normality, of the central figure's psychotic traits. We find similar reflections in some of the minor characters. We recall, for example, that the workman whom Corrado and Giuliana visited at the radar installations had been in 'hospital' with her. We recall also the workman's wife who, in her husband's absence, expresses her opposition to his going to Patagonia. Her unnatural fear of being alone (even for a day, she says) relates clearly to Giuliana's alienation. We are to see Giuliana, then, not merely as a neurotic woman, but as an extreme extension of a general contemporary condition. Virtually the whole film is devoted to the detailed study of her alienation which is offered as the study of the human predicament in an industrialised society.

Il Deserto Rosso is the work of a highly distinguished, subtle and refined sensibility working in a medium whose resources have been completely mastered. All that is best in the film is almost beyond verbal description or analysis. Take the scene in which the hut interior is smashed for firewood: Corrado smashes a partition and later a chair; Giuliana, half frightened, works herself up into a state of extreme nervous exhilaration; then the excitement subsides, and she is left wishing she could always be watching the sea, which never stops moving. The idea, on paper, is perfectly commonplace; the experience conveyed by the movement of the images is not. The sequence communicates a painful awareness of the transience of joy, even at the moment of experiencing it—the 'aching pleasure' of Keats's *Ode on Melancholy*, 'turning to

poison while the bee-mouth sips'. It is one of the moments in the film when Antonioni seems to be groping beyond any concern with the 'modern condition' as such towards more fundamental and permanent metaphysical issues, Giuliana's alienation making her hypersensitive to existence, to time and flux. Antonioni *thinks* here in the movement and rhythms of film as a great poet thinks in the movement and rhythms of verse, 'thinking' here being indistinguishable from feeling. The movements of the actors, the movements of the camera, and the editing, interact to communicate not an intellectual idea but a complete experience. The fact that I could justify my assertion only by quoting is the mark of the completeness of Antonioni's absorption in his medium. Very few directors have developed this ability to think in film, as opposed to translating ideas into images, as thoroughly as he.

One must not, then, object that the visualisation of Giuliana's escape-fantasy (in her story to her son Valerio) is superfluous. Again, it is not the idea that matters but our direct experience of the images: the pan-shot combined with zoom-out that discloses the enormous silent emptiness of sea and rocks contrasted with the noise, dirt and congestion of the industrial reality which surrounds Giuliana. The successive shots of breaking wavelets realise for us her earlier wish to watch the ever-moving sea, and contrast with the image of the polluted water by the docks into which she gazes near the end of the film. Further, this is one of the few sequences in the film that is largely free from apparent colour- and focus-distortions. The soft-focus backgrounds, when used here, serve a specific purpose: simply to suggest Giuliana's focusing of attention on the singing when it begins. Otherwise the only blurrings are the blurrings of distance, and even the slight pink tint of the sand looks natural, as the pink of the bedroom at the end of the love-scene

with Corrado clearly isn't. If one examines the realisation of detail in an Antonioni film at close quarters in this way, one can only admire. It is only when one stands back and looks at the total conception that doubts begin to creep in: when, for instance, one considers the implications of the fact that what the visualisation of the escape-story actually achieves is enormously to strengthen audience identification with Giuliana.

The use of effects or incidents whose interpretation is complex or very uncertain is one of the film's chief characteristics, and partly ac-

Still: Corrado talks to the men about going to work in Patagonia.

counts for its unsettling quality. There is the mysterious scream, for instance (if that is what it is), heard while the party are in the hut. Giuliana and Linda hear it, and *we* hear it, though, at a first viewing, we are very unsure at the point where it is discussed whether we have or not—characteristically, we are put in the position of sharing Giuliana's uncertainty. We must assume, I think, that it is 'real', partly because *both* characters hear it, but more because it is there on the sound-track, without any suggestion that we are to take it as hallucination (as we take the various electronic chords that convey Giuliana's progress towards breakdown, despite their significant resemblance to the industrial noise heard elsewhere in the film). The problem here assumes far greater proportions in *Blow Up*. Yet this takes us no nearer certainty as to its significance. It doesn't sound like a child's cry, and Linda makes no mention of children, yet that is what Giuliana takes it to be. It seems to have no logical connection with the quarantined ship, though the two become linked by association in

Giuliana's mind. There seems to be nowhere the sound could have come from—certainly nowhere in the vicinity that a child might be. But the incident is by no means unrealistic: most of us have heard unexpected sounds which seem to have no discoverable cause, and different people hearing the same sound will interpret it, even *hear* it, differently, according to mood or outlook. For Giuliana the mysterious cry becomes an expression of vulnerability and desolation, it insidiously suggests the vague, inexplicable 'something terrible about reality' that she talks of to Corrado later.

The readiness of Antonioni to present the spectator with incidents of indeterminate significance and leave interpretation open is demonstrated at the outset when Giuliana buys the sandwich from the surprised workman. At least five possible interpretations, each distinct yet all related, are given validity by points in the treatment of the scene and the context of the whole film: 1. The incident straightforwardly establishes Giuliana's condition. Her behaviour, by normal standards irrational, is perfectly logical: she sees the food, feels hungry, and takes the most direct route to appeasing her hunger. This betrays at once her estrangement from the standards of conventional behaviour and her neurotic tendency to let the impulse of the moment override all other considerations (of money; that the man is a total stranger; that the sandwich has been started). 2. She is trying in an ineffectual, neurotic way, to establish contact with her environment by communicating with an industrial worker. 3. Although it is clear that she wants the sandwich for herself, her first action after obtaining it is to offer it to her son. On one level, then, she may be seeking to form a relationship with her child. 4. It is *bread* to which she is so irresistibly attracted,

Still: Giuliana at the docks near the end of Il Deserto Rosso.

114

with its emotional associations of energy and stability, of normal daily life. She is symbolically trying to buy these. 5. She buys it from a *man*, then takes it away and eats it furtively, as if greatly afraid of being discovered. The act then becomes a desperate buying of affection, even of sexual love, of which she feels starved; hence she feels it as a symbolic infidelity, to be surreptitiously and guiltily enjoyed.

All this takes us some way towards defining the sense in which Antonioni can be called an 'instinctive' director. There is no more need for a film-maker than for a poet to have a coherent philosophy underlying his work. On the other hand, Antonioni has frequently been very articulate and definite about his intentions, and clearly one must take some account of this. His pronouncements often seem curiously at variance with the effect of his films: the 'thinker' tends to simplify the artist's complexities. Thus he describes the climax of Giuliana's escape-fantasy, where the girl notices that the rocks are like flesh, in these terms: 'the rocks themselves take on human form, embrace her and sing sweetly'. But there is surely the corollary: for Giuliana, flesh is like rock—other human beings seem impenetrable, inaccessible: true communication is impossible. This interpretation receives ample confirmation at the end of the film where Giuliana, talking to the uncomprehending foreign sailor, tells him of her sense of being 'separate': 'If you prick me, *you* don't feel it'. Besides, the point of the escape-fantasy is surely that if the rocks in some sense 'take on human form', they nonetheless remain rocks. The striking thing about Giuliana's escape world is that it is devoid not merely of industry but of human beings. The mysterious ship that 'braves the seas and storms of this world, and, who knows?, of other worlds' is utterly empty. It somehow fulfils a desire in Giuliana that makes possible a sense of universal harmony, so that '*Everything* was singing'; but it is a harmony that depends on the exclusion of humanity and all the complexities of human interchange.

From Antonioni's interview it emerges that we are to see *Il Deserto Rosso* as being about Giuliana's failure to adjust to the society in which she lives—unexceptionable in itself. But the minor characters, it appears, are to be seen as adjusted to various degrees, and we are to accept them as representing a healthy normality from which Giuliana deviates. It seems to me impossible to do this: the film precisely reverses its creator's expressed intentions. It is also, in its 'instinctive ambiguity', a far richer and more complex work than Antonioni's statements about it would lead one to expect. Apart from Giuliana and Corrado, the characters are all too peripheral for us to get to know very much about them; one gets the feeling that Antonioni is reluctant to examine them closely or in detail. Consequently, we never discover clearly just what their 'adjustment' entails: it seems to amount to little more than an ability to handle machinery and be impervious to noise. Beyond this, the chief characteristic the minor characters reveal is a singular ineffectuality in relationships, an inability, indeed, to form relationships on any but the most superficial level. 'Adjustment' becomes synonymous with insentience. Giuliana's husband Ugo is quite unable to do anything for her and seems, despite one or two tentative advances, indifferent. His attitude to his wife's 'accident', for example (which was really attempted suicide): is he really so insensitive and unperceptive, or does he merely *not want* to know because it would be inconvenient, forcing him into awareness of whole areas of emotional experience his 'adjustment' makes him quite unable to cope with or comprehend? We learn later that he was in London at the time the 'accident' happened, and didn't bother to return home. His chief concern seems to be that Giuliana's opening a shop 'doesn't look right'; he doesn't answer Corrado's 'Why?'. When he finds Giuliana distraught on the landing in the middle of the night—she has dreamed about quicksands, and that the bed was moving—the comfort he can give her is solely a matter of ineffectual caresses: he makes no attempt to understand. The boy Valerio's play with robots and interest in things like exhaust pipes show him presumably to be on the way to a healthy 'adjustment', but he seems on the surface completely unattached. The film leaves us speculating about the *quality* of adult life his adjustment is likely to lead to: amateur, and, indeed, professional, psychologists are all too ready to equate 'adjusted' with 'normal'.

What we have here, in fact, is a treatment in realistic (as opposed to fantasy) terms of a familiar science fiction nightmare, the subject of *Invasion of the Body Snatchers* or *The Thing*

from Another World: the fear of life de-humanized, the fear of the atrophy of emotion. Valerio—the happy and adjusted human being of the future?—is particularly disturbing in this connection. He is a little zombie, about as human as Hawks's 'intellectual carrot'. He brings his mother near to insanity by feigning paralysis, for motives that, like the scream outside the hut, remain obscure: something in him buried deep beyond the possibility of direct expression may be trying to force attention from his mother who, absorbed in her own neurotic condition, mostly neglects him. Yet it is impossible to see in this more than the last vestiges of an all but totally nullified desire for contact. When Giuliana discovers that the illness is a trick, he makes no response whatever to her overwhelming sense of relief, to her impassioned caresses and reproaches. It is from this evidence of a future world without feeling that Giuliana flees to Corrado in the hotel.

The scene of the abortive little would-be orgy in the hut reveals the film's true moral position unequivocally. The cheaply promiscuous pawing and sniggering talk of aphrodisiacs—pornography on the most infantile level—illustrates the trivialising of sex and of human relationships that marks the 'adjusted' characters (Corrado, initially at least, finds it distasteful). After it, Giuliana's straightforward request to her husband to make love comes across as representing a healthy normality, a desire for true intimacy and depth of relationship. Whatever Antonioni may say, it is Giuliana in whom all the film's true positive values are embodied, and in this respect she is consistent with the Monica Vitti characters throughout the tetralogy. In the world Antonioni creates in *Il Deserto Rosso* it is the neurotic and incapable woman who is closest to anything that could be

Stills: Left: '. . . ineffectual caresses . . .'
Right: Giuliana with Valerio.

defended as a tenable 'normality'. Both at the beginning and end of the film she is dressed in a coat of 'natural' green that stands out strongly from the denatured landscape.

The ambivalence of the film appears in the way this feeling for the 'natural' is offset by Antonioni's feeling for the beauty of industrial landscapes. Some very complex emotional effects result from this: consider for example the shot that juxtaposes a small tumbledown hut in a grey-green marshy landscape with the strange inhuman grandeur of the radar installations. The beauty of the factories is set against the fact of river pollution—there is no fishing any more because the fish are all dead or gone away, as the birds learn to live by avoiding the beautiful but poisonous yellow smoke-fumes. The broken-down hut in which the 'orgy' takes place, and where the behaviour, if trivial, is at least a recognisably human intercourse, suggests (with its incongruous picture of zebras) an obsolete, more 'natural' past. When Giuliana asks Corrado what he believes in, his answer is shot in a way that directly expresses this ambivalence. Shown against a natural background, he says he believes 'in a sense' in humanity,

then, with a change in camera position that places him against the pylons, 'in progress'. But 'progress' is destroying nature, 'humanity': the shooting of the scene suggests the incompatibility of Corrado's answers. The beauty of the industrial landscapes takes on an ironic quality in relation to the spiritual poverty of the characters' lives.

The ending of the film, where Giuliana tells Valerio that birds don't get killed flying through the poisonous yellow factory-smoke because they learn to *avoid* it, can scarcely be taken as a simple statement of the need to adjust. It is

Stills: The 'orgy' scene.

rather the summing-up of her final position of total defeat: she will henceforth try to get along, not by coming to terms with her abnormal condition or with her environment (the film's apparent equation of the two here is as revealing as it is unsatisfactory: a point to which I shall return), but simply by blocking them out—by systematically deadening her own responses. Unlike the birds, she can't fly away: she has to live among the objects and sights that are poisonous to her. We see her walking away

119

against a background of factories and yellow containers that is again an out-of-focus blur. The very last shot of the film, which immediately follows, shows us the same factories in focus. The intention, presumably, was to convey to the spectator a sense of release not shared by the protagonist (like the last shot of *Psycho*). The effect is converted into one of bitter despair, by the loathing of industrialism on human grounds that the film has by now defined; this is scarcely mitigated by the feeling for the *aesthetic* beauty of factories. In the background rises the poisoned yellow smoke, and the sense of the parable is surely clear: to avoid it is to live a life of spiritual paralysis, to accept it is to die. The choice we are offered is between Ugo, Valerio and adjustment on the one hand, and Giuliana on the other. Once one has discarded Antonioni's pronouncements and grasped that the core of the film is a total pessimism, *Il Deserto Rosso* becomes consistent in its ambivalence. There remain, I think, some quite fundamental objections to be made, perhaps not unrelated to this lack of self-awareness which is curious in so intelligent and sensitive an artist.

Hitchcock and Antonioni would not at first, or indeed at second sight, appear to have much in common; but their work offers two of the most fully developed manifestations of 'pure cinema'. Both use the cinema primarily to convey emotional experience directly to the audience; when two roughly contemporaneous films have as their core the experiences of a highly neurotic woman, comparisons become interesting. I am not the first critic to comment on the resemblance between the red suffusions in *Marnie* and Antonioni's use of soft-focus backgrounds, to communicate what the heroine is feeling while keeping her in the image: a compression of the familiar technique of close-up followed by subjective shot. The red suffusions seem at first insufferably crude beside the subtle and delicate effects of colour and tone achieved by Antonioni and his cameraman Carlo di Palma. But their function is really quite different: the red suffusions in *Marnie* are a means to an end, whereas in Antonioni the subjective effects become virtually an end in themselves.

The closest parallel with *Marnie* is offered, not by the soft focus (used to suggest Giuliana's general condition), but by the occasional use of colour distortions: the grey fruit on the stall outside Giuliana's shop, the white hotel interior (with white foliage on the rubber plants), the suddenly pink bedroom after the love-making with Corrado. These, like Marnie's red suffusions, occur only at stress-crises: the grey fruit after Giuliana's confrontation with Corrado in the shop has brought to the surface all her doubts about her ability to cope actively with existence; the white interior after her grip on reality (and her desire to maintain it) has been undermined by the incident of Valerio's feigned paralysis. The pink bedroom, with its jarring unnaturalness, comes across as an hysterical hallucination after Corrado's wretched failure to appease her anguish by making love to her. One of the film's most disturbing emotional effects is achieved in this shot (which some critics have found merely 'vulgar'), which fuses several contradictory responses: the *real* bedroom becomes an *unnatural* pink that recalls the *natural* pink of the *fantasy* beach. It is for Giuliana at once a desperate attempt to comfort herself and an image of unnerving unreality. Its bewildering ambiguity is juxtaposed with the ominous electronic chord that suggests the imminence of insanity. These colour distortions (or simplifications) are Giuliana's means of neutralising the pressures of existence—her sense that 'everything hurts' (as in the escape-fantasy 'everything sings'). The monochrome has at once the effect of holding reality at a distance and simplifying it, hence making it bearable: the direct opposite of Marnie's panic reactions to red. The comparison reveals something important about *Il Deserto Rosso* when one considers the difference between the effects of these devices on the spectator. The very directness of the effect—the crudity, if you like —links the red suffusions (however strong their 'panic' effect on the audience) unequivocally with Marnie's subjective impressions: they are too *obviously* stylised for us to mistake them for reality. In their subtlety of presentation, and in their realism—Antonioni had the fruit and the plants actually painted, so there is no photographic trickery—the colour distortions in *Il Deserto Rosso* come across as rather more than merely Giuliana's hallucinations: they go some way towards imposing her neurotic view of existence on the spectator, and in this again that view tends dangerously to become the positive centre of the film.

Any attempt at re-creating in terms of colour and image complex inner emotional states must *necessarily* be inadequate: no change in the

Photograph: Monica Vitti beside the stall of grey fruit.

appearance of the external world can entirely convey the inner experience of alienation, though Antonioni achieves some haunting effects. Hitchcock's red, on the other hand, simply because it *is* unashamedly crude and direct, is a perfectly acceptable shorthand to suggest to us all those details of neurotic symptoms that his film is only incidentally concerned with. Hitchcock is concerned singlemindedly with cure and consequently with cause, the clinical details of Marnie's case being reduced to the barest essentials, though with all manner of complexities implied. Antonioni character-

istically gives us an elaborate display of symptoms. For all its stylisation, *Il Deserto Rosso* is much the more naturalistic of the two films, because it is concerned far more with the details of neurotic *behaviour*. Cause, in fact, is entirely ignored; or, rather, the film leaves us to infer (by its refusal to offer any alternative) that 'inability to adjust' *is* the cause rather than the effect of Giuliana's condition. This is not a new trick. As long ago as 1797, in a poem called *Frost at Midnight*, the author of *The Ancient Mariner* tried to convince himself (under Wordsworth's influence) that his complicated and deeply disturbed condition was the result of having been brought up in a city instead of among the mountains of the Lake District. Similarly, Antonioni is too ready to blame 'modern conditions'. One was never wholly convinced in *L'Avventura* that Sandro's failure as a human being was entirely explicable in the terms proposed. In *Il Deserto Rosso* we never really accept industrialism as sufficient explanation of Giuliana's condition, and are left wondering whether she would be able to adjust to *any* milieu. Whereupon the whole ostensible subject of the film crumbles away, and we are left asking ourselves, '*Why* a neurotic for protagonist?'. Antonioni anticipates these objections in the interview referred to earlier, but I don't think he adequately answers them.

The somewhat enervating effect of much of Antonioni's recent work seems to be intimately connected with the split between conscious and unconscious intentions. In *Il Deserto Rosso* the complex of tendencies analysable in the films from *L'Avventura* on reaches its culmination in some respects and begins to be transcended

Stills: Corrado makes love to Giuliana.

in others. Here the enervating effect of self-conscious insistence on style is offset by the constant fertility of invention and the readiness to leave things relatively open (in details if not in overall sense). This, and Monica Vitti's inherent vitality, make the film far more exciting to watch than *La Notte*. But to centre a statement about the contemporary condition on a highly, perhaps incurably neurotic woman who is unable even to begin coping with her situation, unable to draw upon any insight or awareness, and to reduce the other characters to ciphers, is again to make things too easy. What

Penelope Houston called 'unresolved tensions' in the film amount to spiritual deadlock, and, given the director's ambivalent (or confused?) attitude to his subject-matter, Giuliana was perhaps the only kind of protagonist possible. One of the consequences is a singular lack of development within the film. The ending makes it clear that Giuliana hasn't made any significant progress, a point emphasized by the fact that she is dressed as she was at the beginning.

Still: Disturbed by the arrival of the quarantined ship, Giuliana nearly kills herself.

BLOW UP

If not the greatest, *Blow Up* seems to me easily the most likeable of Antonioni's later films; and its freshness and vivacity make one look forward to his future work with an eagerness one would scarcely have anticipated in the days of *La Notte* and *L'Eclisse*.

Il Deserto Rosso marked a break with the past in comparatively peripheral ways; *Blow Up* makes the break more extreme and decisive. The change of country, change of language and change of star in themselves suggest a conscious determination to make a new beginning. What vitality the last four films possessed had its primary centre in Monica Vitti. Nonetheless, one had come to feel that she and Antonioni were not doing each other (artistically speaking) much good. One doesn't blame Miss Vitti for this, nor for the unhappy fact that the break-away, for her, took the form of Mr Losey and *Modesty Blaise* (someone should have introduced her to Howard Hawks). Even in *L'Avventura* and *La Notte* the woman's frustrations had been the emotional core of the film; *L'Eclisse* and *Il Deserto Rosso* carried this tendency to its logical conclusion by making the woman unequivocally the central consciousness through whose medium each film is experienced. This habit of building films around the frustrations of a central female figure was becoming inseparable from Antonioni's use of Monica Vitti as star. The crucial development in *Blow Up* is the shift to a male protagonist; though it is probably owing to this shift that the film lacks the emotional weight of its forerunners.

What one first notices about *Blow Up* is its tempo, its effect of spontaneity, its lack of mannerisms. Where *La Notte*, for example, seems much longer than it really is, *Blow Up* seems shorter. The preoccupation with beauty of style as an end in itself that characterized the preceding films is largely absent. The cleanness and directness of expression in *Blow Up* suggests a much more immediate (hence for Antonioni healthier, because less self-conscious) involvement with the subject matter. Although the adventurous and experimental use of colour in *Il Deserto Rosso* gave that film its continuously alive surface, one can also feel that the far more straightforward and unfussy (though often very striking and bold) use of colour in *Blow Up* is further evidence of this. The generally brisk tempo, the feeling of spontaneity, and more specifically the lively and nervous editing with occasional jump-cuts (e.g., in Thomas's drive to the junk-shop) suggest that the New Wave has been, if nothing so definite as an influence, at least an important stimulus. The spirit of enquiry and exploration foreshadowed in certain aspects of the previous film is a much stronger determinant in *Blow Up*, and this is surely closely connected with the new hero-figure. Antonioni here sets out to examine how a man can try to live in the more 'advanced' environments of modern civilisation, instead of starting from the assumption that he can't. Or that, at least, is about half the truth.

Blow Up has been adversely criticized in Britain on the grounds that Antonioni's picture of an anyway largely mythical 'Swinging London' falls somewhat short of objective documentary verisimilitude; or that he has seized only on its most obvious and superficial aspects; or that he has been guilty of a sort of arty-commercial sensationalism (the nude romp with the teenage girls; the drug party). The first of these objections need bother us no more than complaints that *King Lear* has its shortcomings if judged as a documentary portrait of prehistoric Britain. It is true that Antonioni's previous films have shown a very strong and sensitive response to the Spirit of Place, and that his use of particular localities and their atmosphere counts for quite a lot in their emotional effect. But Place has never been of *essential* importance to the concerns of his films—those concerns would not be fundamentally affected by transplantation to other cities or other countries. Even if the world of *Blow Up* were demonstrably a fantasy creation, this would not invalidate the film in the least: Antonioni would not be the first artist to treat essential reality through the medium of fantasy. But it seems to me that Antonioni's depiction of contemporary London doesn't go beyond the simplification and intensification of accepted artistic method. One might accuse the Yardbirds sequence of distorting reality, and the appearance of the Rag Week mime group in the last scene clearly works only on a symbolic level; otherwise, Antonioni's method seems one of selection rather than falsification. As to the other objections, it is a great mistake to equate 'obvious' with 'superficial': the most obvious aspects of a society are very likely to be also among its most important. The artist concerned with the way civilisation is moving will necessarily have to deal with extremes, in which forward-pointing tendencies are likely to be expressed. Simply to show nude romps and drug orgies is not necessarily to sell out to commercialism: it depends entirely on their relation to the whole.

Antonioni's later films are built not so much on plots as on cumulative episodes, linked by a common theme or principle of composition. In *Blow Up* he uses a classic mystery-thriller plot, but uses it only as one element—albeit a central one—in the whole. The form of the film can be compared to a Theme-and-Variations, bearing in mind that all the best sets of variations are not merely strung together like beads, but have a cumulative effect. The underlying principle of composition on which the whole film is built is given with diagrammatic simplicity in the credit-titles. The credit sequences in Antonioni's recent work commonly have a function of this kind: one thinks of the contrast in music (strident 'pop' and menacing serialism) that epitomises the world of *L'Eclisse,* the soft-focus industrial scenes and the wordless 'escape' song that epitomise the complementary sides of Giuliana's existence in *Il Deserto Rosso. Blow Up* begins with grass. Through the printed letters of the titles we see a model or starlet striking erotic poses for photographers. At once a simple and basic reality is set against the corrupting artificiality and falsity of the modern commercial world. As we watch, we become aware of a curious effect. If we concentrate on the grass, the credits appear to be imposed on it as on a solid; as soon as we concentrate on the lettering, it appears like patterned windows cut into the grass (which becomes a mere façade) revealing the gesturing girl behind. So, at the outset, we are presented with a simple ambiguity in spatial relationships that undermines our confidence in our own perceptions, our certainty about what is real.

Ambiguity, uncertainty, the blurring of distinctions, inform every episode in the film. Far from attempting a documentary examination of London, Antonioni selects only what is relevant to this central compositional principle, so that even the most incidental details fall naturally into place in the total picture. Nothing is definitively identifiable: outside the junkshop Thomas sees two feminine-looking men walking poodles, and shortly after, in the park, a masculine-looking woman in male uniform picking up litter with a pointed stick. Nothing is quite what it looks like: the façade of Thomas's house/studio seems to have no relation to the world behind it, the restaurant where he goes for lunch is indistinguishable from a private house. Objects are separated from their functions, or become wildly incongruous with the environments in which they are placed or the human behaviour around them: a propeller becomes an ungainly ornament that may 'break up that straight line', an alabaster bust of a girl in lace coyly surveys the varieties of erotic behaviour in Thomas's studio, the drug orgy takes place among antique furniture and Victorian and Edwardian paintings and busts. Painting reflects this shifting reality by becoming indeterminate: Antonioni has repeatedly used abstract art to suggest modern man's up-

rootedness and instability (see, for example, the art exhibition Claudia visits in *L'Avventura* to pass the time while Sandro and Anna make what passes for love; or the paintings that surround and seem to press in on the ex-lovers in Riccardo's apartment at the beginning of *L'Eclisse*). The artist in *Blow Up* can make no sense of his abstracts until he has finished painting them; the painting Thomas wants to buy or be given is, significantly, one that the artist hasn't yet identified. What Antonioni

Still: Thomas, the artist and the picture.

takes from London is its cosmopolitanism, and the surrealistic incongruities that can spring from it: one shot near the beginning of the film juxtaposes coloured nuns, guardsmen in bus-bies, and Rag Week students in clown make-up, in an image of naturalistically feasible unreality. No one has any sense of *positive* purpose: even the posters in the protest march with which Thomas, driving from the restaurant, gets tangentially involved, are exclusively negative. Most of them simply say 'NO'; some are upside down ('ON'), therefore meaningless or contra-dictory. Any doubts that Giuliana's vision of

existence in *Il Deserto Rosso* was essentially shared by her creator should be decisively removed by *Blow Up*, which is singlemindedly concerned with life on quicksand.

As we move in from the peripheries towards the centre of the film, we find everywhere varia-tions on this basic principle. Consider, for instance, the women: the artist's mistress (wife? —even the relationship is uncertain), and the girl who owns the junk-shop (I shall examine the role of the Vanessa Redgrave character later). Sarah Miles's part is said to have been reduced somewhat in the editing of the film, and some have found its undefined nature a weakness; surely the cuts were made to *increase* the character's enigmatic quality? We see her, after all, as we see nearly everything, from Thomas's viewpoint, and it is sufficiently clear that Antonioni isn't cheating—nothing *essential* about her that Thomas knows is being withheld from the spectator. Near the end, after Thomas has eavesdropped on her (or more accurately her lover's) love-making, she comes to ask his advice; but it quickly becomes apparent that she doesn't even know what she wants to ask, and can tell him nothing relevant as she is un-able to formulate it even to herself. She and the girl in the junk-shop are more fully crystallised reflections of the uncertainty that is developing within Thomas. The junk-shop girl exists amongst a litter of dusty, chipped and obsolete bric-à-brac that suggests her rootlessness. She is selling the shop in order to go abroad and find something else—Nepal, perhaps. Thomas tells her Nepal is full of antiques. Morocco, then.

Relationships in the world of *Blow Up* are unstable, enigmatic or deceptive. Sarah Miles lives with Thomas's artist friend yet seems on intimate terms with Thomas, who fondles her in front of her lover. When Thomas sees the

Still: David Hemmings and Sarah Miles.

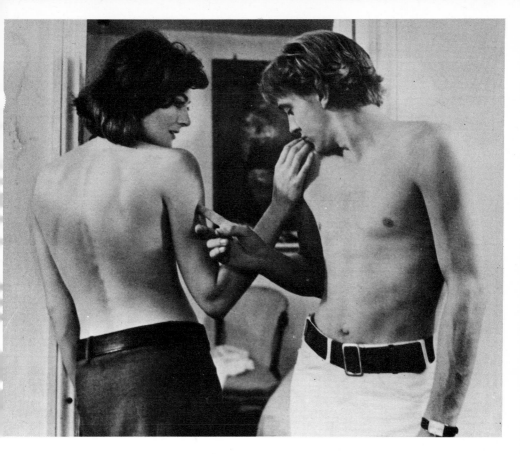

artist making love to her, she is making no response whatever—she seems to be merely
allowing him to use her to work himself off. The
relationship gives her no sense of identity, or of
belonging. The relationship between Vanessa
Redgrave and the man in the park is almost
(but not quite) certainly not what it looks like.
And what of her relationship with Thomas?
When she finds she can't get the photos he has
taken of her in any other way, she begins to

Still: Ambiguous motivation in Blow Up: *Vanessa Redgrave and David Hemmings.*

take off her clothes. He stops her, and gives her
a roll of film she thinks is the one she wants (it
isn't); whereupon she *continues* her attempt to
seduce him. So where does her interest in
getting the film end and her interest in having
Thomas make love to her begin? Clearly, there
is no answer.

129

In a life of quicksands, purpose falters, deviates, collapses. Thomas goes to negotiate to buy a junk-shop, sees a huge wooden propeller, and, in the excitement of buying it, goes off with the original purpose relegated to the background. Vanessa Redgrave comes for a roll of film and stays to make love; then this purpose, too, interrupted by the delivery of the propeller, comes to nothing. Thomas's fascinated investigation of the evidence of his photographs gives

Still: Erotic photographing.

way easily enough to the distractions offered by two teenage girls; the girls, who came to pose for photographs, are quickly diverted into coffee-making and a sex-romp, by the end of which Thomas is too 'whacked' to do more than shunt them off until tomorrow. Thomas's discovery of a murder elicits some interest from Sarah Miles, but not enough for her to do anything or give him any real support; the editor of his book of photographs (Ron) isn't roused by it sufficiently to break off his withdrawl into drugs for the evening. Earlier, in the restaurant, Thomas expressed his desire for 'tons of money'—'Then I'd be free.' 'Free to do what?', Ron asked. 'Free like him?'—indicating one of Thomas's photographs. Without roots, without purpose, without identity, the image of freedom becomes a bleary and disturbed alcoholic on a wasteground—or a drug orgy.

The distinction between appearance and reality blurs and dissolves. Thomas's photographing of an erotically twisting and writhing model becomes not only a substitute for sexual intercourse but virtually indistinguishable from it. In the course of it Thomas sprawls over her, kisses her, shouts erotic exhortations ('Yes, yes, more! More! Give it me . . .' etc.); at the end the 'lovers' both sink back exhausted, apparently satisfied, as after orgasm. All sense of values disintegrates: the electric guitar smashed during the Yardbirds' number is one minute a trophy to be hysterically battled for, the next a bit of rubbish to be kicked aside into the gutter.

One of the first things Vanessa Redgrave says to Thomas in the park is 'No, we haven't met—you've never seen me.' The invitation to deliberate prevarication or suppression takes on far more sinister overtones as the film progresses. The main drift of *Blow Up* seems to me very clear: we are shown a young man inhabiting a world in which everything combines to undermine the firmness of his hold on reality. The mystery surrounding the murder comes as a test: he is subjected to a *deliberate* undermining of his confidence in his own perceptions, and he crumbles. The cumulative effect of the episodes (or variations), both on Thomas and on the spectator, should also be clear, with various points quite unconnected with the mystery-thriller narrative (Thomas's failure to answer Ron's 'Free like him?'; his joining in the battle for the guitar) acting as landmarks in the protagonist's development. The murder is, nonetheless, at the core of the film.

I know intelligent people who deny that there is a murder at all, except in Thomas's fantasy. This theory seems to me chiefly interesting in its unwitting confirmation of the universality of the film's theme—that we are all in danger of losing our grasp of objective reality—but it had better be answered briefly. It takes two forms: (a) Everything that happens in the park, everything involved in the mystery, is fantasy; (b) only the body is fantasy—the rest really happened, but Thomas misinterpreted his pictures and then hallucinated the corpse. The chief argument underlying the former seems to be that no one but Thomas sees Vanessa Redgrave or the body, or notices the photographs (which are hanging up during the scene with the teenage girls). It quickly reveals its full absurdity if one just pursues it logically: the murder is fantasy, Vanessa Redgrave is fantasy, her lover is fantasy, Thomas's photographing of them is fantasy, the park (perhaps) is fantasy; then the developing and printing of the photos is fantasy; the pictures hanging round the walls during the romp with the teenagers is fantasy, the theft of the photos is fantasy, the print the thieves leave behind is fantasy. No psychological theory of fantasy-making could possibly cope with all that, and it obviously makes no artistic sense whatever. The latter objection also (but less decisively) destroys the far more interesting second hypothesis. At the end of the film Thomas hallucinates the sound (at least) of a tennis ball hit by a racquet. This hallucination is the film's logical climax, and marks a decisive stage in the character's evolution; consequently, for him to have had a far more extreme hallucination much earlier would entirely destroy the film's logic. Above all, we must surely trust the director. When Thomas hallucinates the tennis-ball, Antonioni shows us unequivocally that there is no tennis-ball there, and introduces the sound in such a way as to indicate clearly that it is subjective; when Thomas sees the corpse, we see it too, and there is no hint that we shouldn't be seeing it. Further, we see the corpse when Thomas doesn't see it, as he photographs Vanessa Redgrave walking away from him past it. We see it in too distant long-shot, admittedly, to be sure what it is or even to notice it at the time: the shot provides a cinematic equivalent for Thomas's blurred blow-up, which would not be acceptable as police-court evidence. But what is at issue is not police-court evidence but our confidence in our perceptions, and a second viewing of the film will convince anyone that the corpse is lying where Thomas later sees it at the end of the first park scene. The incident closely parallels the mysterious scream in *Il Deserto Rosso*, which the spectator hears and which Monica Vitti hears: her certainty that she has heard it is later undermined, and ours with it, but the scream is there on the sound-track just as the body is there on the screen, and in doubting the reality of either we are merely

aligning ourselves with the characters' break-downs. Since in many respects the films encourage us to do precisely this, it is particularly important to cling on firmly to what rocks in the quicksand they offer.

There *is* a murder, then. Thomas unwittingly photographs both the corpse and the murderer, and later sees the corpse. He comes to doubt its reality, and our own certainty is undermined, but he is wrong and we are wrong: that is the point. We can deduce with fair certainty—as

Stills: Blow Up.

he does—what has happened: Vanessa Redgrave has lured the man to the pre-arranged place where he is to be shot; one photograph (the one indeed that provides Thomas with his first clue) shows her looking anxiously towards the fence behind which the killer is hiding. When she sees Thomas taking the films she pleads with him to give them to her. He refuses, and he photographs her again as she hurries away: she in fact pauses by the corpse with a startled gesture (not expecting that the crime, after the interruption, could have been carried out? Not expecting the corpse to be in that

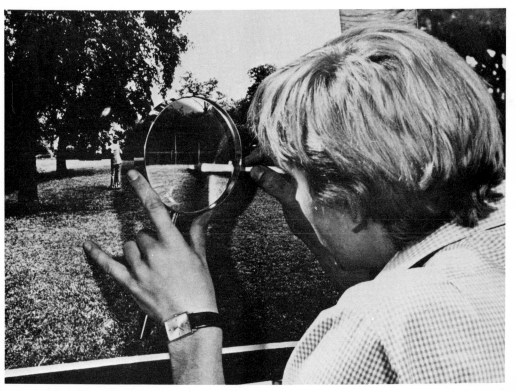

position? Afraid because it is so inadequately concealed? Horrified at what she has connived at?) and then runs on out of view. Later, while Thomas is in the restaurant ordering a meal he characteristically never eats, a man (the killer? another accomplice?) tries to steal the roll of film from his car. Later still Vanessa Redgrave confronts Thomas at his studio and is given a false roll of film by him. Finally, the studio is ransacked and all the prints

removed except for one enlargement of the corpse, blown up so that, as Sarah Miles says, it is scarcely distinguishable from the artist's abstract paintings. Antonioni convinces us of the extreme probability of this interpretation of events, and at the same time shows us Thomas's increasing distrust of his own per-

Stills: Above: the false roll of film; right, Thomas studies his blow-ups.

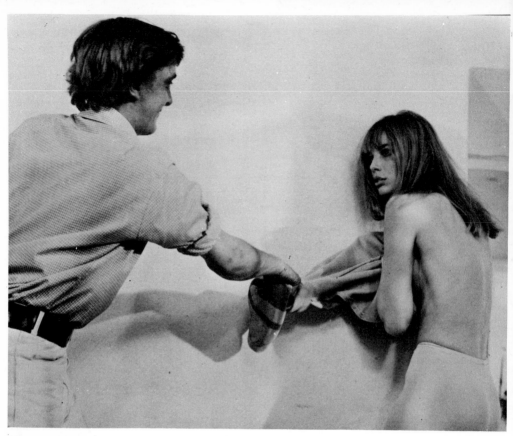

ceptions. 'Extreme probability'—the interpretation isn't susceptible of proof, and it is just possible to construct a theory, far-fetched but feasible, that covers the available evidence and makes Vanessa Redgrave innocent (of the murder, at least!): she is genuinely out with her lover, and her private life is, as she later tells Thomas, already a mess; she looks at the bushes because she glimpses a movement there; she does nothing about the killing because she can't afford to be implicated.

The obvious question, Why doesn't Thomas tell the police?, is not, I think, to be dismissed as one of those Awkward Questions on the suppression of which the continuance of the plot depends. Antonioni encourages us to ask it, by having it raised in the film and left unanswered (during Thomas's conversation with Sarah Miles). In fact, in the context of the mood and concerns of the film as a whole, the question seems immediately risible: one thinks of Hitchcock's policeman in *The Birds* solemnly identifying as a sparrow one small feathered corpse among the thousands littering the shattered parlour, forerunner perhaps of a shattered world. The police are of no relevance to Thomas (or to the film) because Thomas is not concerned with justice. Nowhere does he show any *moral* concern about the murder. Moral distinctions in the quicksand world of *Blow Up* are as blurred as any others, and definitions such as 'Good' and 'Wicked' cease to have validity or even meaning. Legal proceedings would categorize the Vanessa Redgrave character very precisely as 'Murderer's Accomplice', while we see, with Thomas, an evidently very complicated and bewildered, and highly sensitive and vulnerable, human being.

The notorious episode with the teenage girls is relevant here. No one wants to admit to being

Stills: Left: the beginning of the nude romp with the teenagers; below: 'Thomas's interest returns to the photographs . . . .'

shocked by it, but lots of people profess to be shocked that Antonioni should try so hard to shock us. Surely the shocking thing about the scene is that it isn't presented as shocking? In fact, it is very funny and charming. Uncertainty as to what exactly *happens* is not Antonioni's fault (I understand that the version shown in Sweden continues beyond the British version); but the shot that follows the abrupt cutting-off of festivities, of Thomas being dressed by the two now very subservient young ladies, clearly implies that he has established himself as their lord and master. The film expresses no disapproval: the spectator is left free to contemplate a total breakdown of traditional moral assumptions. As the girls dress him, Thomas's interest returns to the photographs suspended around them, as if what has intervened has, in some indirect way, led his attention back to them.

What becomes of first importance to Thomas

is not abstract justice but something very concrete and personal. With his hold on reality weakening, he must get a picture of the corpse; in other words, he must *know* that he has seen what he has seen. Alternatively (or, better still, as well) he must share his knowledge with another consciousness. The importance these aims assume is the index of the weakening of Thomas's own confidence. The drug orgy amid which he finds Ron and into which he himself (we presume) is finally drawn, is not a bit of cheap sensationalism nor a bit of spurious local colour in the 'Swinging London' scene. It is the logical culmination of a film, constructed like a poem of thematically related images, about the way in which perceptions can be tampered with, undermined, and finally broken down. Thomas emerges from it at dawn with his camera, but it is too late—the corpse, and with it Thomas's last chance to prove to himself the reality of what he has seen, has gone.

Finding my response to the Rag Week students somewhat at odds with that of others, I have been prepared to find there an interesting ambiguity. In vain: subsequent viewings merely confirm original impressions. The students are introduced at the beginning of the film, driving round and round a deserted space enclosed by tall office blocks, hectically shouting and gesturing with frenetic gaiety to an audience which isn't there: an image suggesting at once their unreality and ineffectuality. Their reappearance at the end is difficult to explain in naturalistic terms, and must be taken symbolically, as the logical outcome of what we have been shown. In the surrounding reality of grass and trees the white painted faces look grotesque and deathly; the faces of the 'spectators', pressed against the netting of the tennis court to follow an imaginary ball, are the faces of the lost. Thomas's retrieving of the 'ball' marks his final surrender: his grasp of objective reality fatally undermined, he is a lost (because dis-integrated) soul. His face is that of a man near the verge of insanity. The last two shots of the film show him (a) in long-shot against a great stretch of grass, diminished and alone, and (b) disappeared. The film ends, as it began, with the simple reality of growing grass which, like Giuliana's escape-ship and escape-island, has no human complications to make existence a quicksand, but which, unlike Giuliana's island, at least *exists*, and is there, unequivocally, for us to contemplate. Thomas no longer exists.

Although a slight figure (whose slightness accounts for that of the film of which he is the dominating consciousness), Thomas is a far more active and positive figure than most of Antonioni's male protagonists, and his defeat accordingly seems at first to carry that much more weight. At the same time his very activeness is to some extent at odds with the drift of the film as a whole: we are not at the end really convinced that so chirpy and resilient a man would be so decisively undermined by the experiences we are shown him undergoing. Isn't Antonioni manipulating the character against its nature, in order, once again, to bring the film round to a final and too easy defeat? There remains some conflict between the traditional plot-and-character narrative at the core of the film and the more typically Antonionian 'poetic' form of thematically related episodes and images. The latter is, as usual, contrived to express a predetermined defeat, and plot and character are forced to submit, even though they seem to want to develop more 'openly'. The artist's description in the film of how his paintings develop, spontaneously and subconsciously, so that it is only later, by finding a clue and following it, that he understands them, is probably intended as a 'testament' description of how Antonioni makes his films, and one

Still: Vanessa Redgrave tries to prevent Thomas from photographing her in the park.

can see that their 'variation' form of related episodes supports this. But this doesn't really contradict the 'predetermined' effect of his films—predetermination can as easily work subconsciously as deliberately, *more* easily, perhaps, when it remains unchecked by fully conscious recognition. Antonioni has found a more 'open' hero, but he is still incapable of making a truly 'open' film—as one sees immediately if one sets *Blow Up* beside another film about contemporary bewilderment and confusion, Godard's *Une Femme Mariée*. One can point here to the Yardbirds scene, and Antonioni's presentation of the audience in the 'pop' cellar. Are such audiences, in anybody's experience, composed of immovable and near-expressionless zombies? It might be defended, I suppose, as a 'poetic' image intended to reveal an essential reality, and to mark a stage in Thomas's descent; to me it seems another example of Antonioni's manipulation of reality to express an easy defeat, and strangely at odds with the genuinely 'open' scene with the teenage girls.

Like *Il Deserto Rosso*, *Blow Up* tries to make a clear distinction between objective reality and its protagonist's failure to maintain his grasp of it. The last shots of the two films are closely parallel: Giuliana walks past out-of-focus factories and stockyards, which Antonioni slides *into* focus for us to contemplate as they really are; Thomas's confidence in his perceptions of reality have collapsed, but *we* are left to contemplate the real grass. Yet in both films the characters' breakdown carries weight disproportionate to the 'placing' of that breakdown: there remains grave doubt whether the encouragement to share the central figures' disturbed vision doesn't greatly outweigh any attempts to detach us from its distortions and limitations. During *Blow Up*'s final tennis-match, the camera-movements follow the imaginary ball's trajectory so as to place the audience subjectively in the hallucinated position of Thomas and the mime group, just as in *Il Deserto Rosso*, through the use of soft-focus and colour distortions, the audience participates in Giuliana's alienation. This in itself can be readily enough defended as honesty on Antonioni's part—Giuliana and Thomas, if extreme cases, are to be taken as to some extent representative modern consciousnesses, not clearly distinguishable from ourselves and the director, and the films derive their force from this. It is less defensible when placed in the context of Antonioni's tendency to manipulate his films towards a pre-ordained defeat. The overall effect of Antonioni's films is still to limit rather than extend the spectator's sense of the possibilities of life.

One wonders too what effect the move from Italy (if permanent) is going to have on Antonioni. Ridiculous as I find the complaint that *Blow Up* doesn't offer a very faithful picture of London life, the fact remains that, however related to modern experience thematically, the film exists in a vacuum, and there can be great dangers for the artist in this, the chief being that of finally losing all contact with any sense of human normality (real or potential). For all that, *Blow Up* remains a consistently exciting and stimulating work, and one is both surprised and delighted to be using such words of a film by the author of *La Notte*. It has been said that *Blow Up* is incomprehensible to the older generation and immediately accessible to the younger. This is an exaggeration (at least one middle-aged schoolmaster—myself—had to explain parts of it to some of his pupils), but it contains some truth, and this is greatly to Antonioni's credit. It joins a handful of works (Ionesco's *Tueur sans Gages*, *Une Femme Mariée*, *Persona*—though it is less completely satisfying than any of these) which really express for me what it feels like to be alive today.

FILMOGRAPHY

Born 29th September, 1912 at Ferrara in Tuscany. Studied in the Faculty of Economics and Commerce at the University of Bologna. During studies and after wrote for a newspaper in Ferrara, 'Il Corriere Padano'. Became interested in cinema and theatre and started making a 16mm. documentary in a mental hospital. Worked in a bank after obtaining his degree in 1935, but left the job to move to Rome in 1939. There he contributed to the magazine 'Cinema', edited by Vittorio Mussolini, the dictator's son. Other contributors were Barbaro, Pasinetti and Zavattini. In 1940-41 enrolled as a student of directing at the Centro Sperimentale di Cinematografia but remained only for some months. Continued writing occasional articles until 1949—bibliographies of these are to be found in the books by Leprohon and Bernardini.

Assistant director
1942: *I Due Foscari*. Directed by Enrico Fulchignoni.
1942: *Les Visiteurs du soir*. Directed by Marcel Carné.

Scriptwriter
1942: *I Due Foscari* in collaboration with G. Campanile Mancini, Mino Doletti, Enrico Fulchignoni.
1942: *Un Pilota ritorna* in collaboration with Rosario Leone, Ugo Betti, Massimo Mida, Gherardo Gherardi. Directed by Roberto Rossellini.
1947: *Caccia Tragica* in collaboration with Giuseppe De Santis, Carlo Lizzani, Cesare Zavattini, Corrado Alvaro, Umberto Barbaro, Tullio Pinelli. Directed by Giuseppe De Santis.
1952: *Le Sciecco Bianco (The White Sheik)* in collaboration with Federico Fellini, Tullio Pinelli. Directed by Federico Fellini.

Short films as writer/director
1943-47: GENTE DEL PO
Production: I.C.E.T. Photographed by Piero Portalupi. Music by Mario Labroca. Edited by C. A. Chiesa. 9 minutes.
The voyage of a barge down the River Po. A documentary on the villages on the banks of the Po and the people who lived in them. Partly lost in processing and partly destroyed by humidity when the negative was stored during the last years of the war, the final version was edited in 1947 from barely half the original footage.

1948: N.U.—*Nettezza Urbana*
Production: I.C.E.T. Photographed by Giovanni Ventimiglia. Music by Giovanni Fusco. 9 minutes.

A day in the life of Rome's street cleaners, filmed chronologically from dawn to dusk.

1948: SUPERSTIZIONE—*Non ci credo!*
Production: I.C.E.T. Photographed by Giovanni Ventimiglia. Music by Giovanni Fusco. 9 minutes.
A catalogue of illegal superstitious practices in a small village near Camerino in the Marches. Final version is not as Antonioni intended because the producer compelled him to return to Rome before shooting was completed.

1948-49: L'AMOROSA MENZOGNA
Production: Filmus. Photographed by Renato del Frate. Music by Giovanni Fusco. Assistant director: Francesco Maselli. 10 minutes. With: Anna Vita, Sergio Raimondi, Annie O'Hara, Sandro Roberti.
The life of the stars of the *fumetti*, photographed comic strips, in contrast to their public images.

1950: SETTE CANNE, UN VESTITO
Production: I.C.E.T. Photographed by Giovanni Ventimiglia. Stock music. 10 minutes.
A documentary on the manufacture of rayon, shot in Torviscosa, near Trieste.

1950: LA VILLA DEI MOSTRI
Production: Filmus. Photographed by Giovanni De Paoli. Music by Giovanni Fusco. 10 minutes.
Sculptures of monstrous human figures in the park of an ancient villa at Bomarzo, near Viterbo.

1950: LA FUNIVIA DEL FALORIA
Production: Theo Usuelli. Photographed by Goffredo Bellisario, Ghedina. Music by Theo Usuelli. 10 minutes.
The cable railway that runs between Cortina d'Ampezzo and Mount Faloria. Antonioni was unable to make the film which he had planned because of a drastic reduction in budget. He returned to Rome for conferences on the making of a feature.

Feature films as director
1950: CRONACA DI UN AMORE
Production: Villani Film (Franco Villani, Stefano Caretta). Screenplay by Antonioni, Daniele D'Anza, Silvio Giovaninetti, Francesco Maselli, Piero Tellini, from a story by Antonioni. Photographed by Enzo Serafin. Sets by Piero Filippone. Costumes for Lucia Bosè by Ferdinando Sarmi. Music by Giovanni Fusco (solo saxophone: Marcel Mule). Assistant Director:

Francesco Maselli. Director of Production: Gino Rossi. Shot in and around Milan. First shown: Biarritz Film Festival, October, 1950. Première: Rome, November 25th, 1950. 96 minutes.

With: Lucia Bosè (Paola Molon), Massimo Girotti (Guido), Ferdinando Sarmi (Enrico Fontana), Gino Rossi (detective), Marika Rowsky (model), Rosi Mirafiore (barmaid), Rubi D'Alma.

1952: I VINTI
Production: Film Costellazione, S.G.C.(Paris). Story and screenplay: Antonioni, Suso Cecchi D'Amico, Giorgio Bassani, Diego Fabbri, Turi Vasile, Roger Nimier (French episode). Photographed by Enzo Serafin. Sets by Gianni Polidori. Music by Giovanni Fusco. Edited by Eraldo Da Roma. Assistant Directors: Francesco Rosi, Alain Cuny. Director of Production: Paolo Moffa. Shot in Rome, London, Paris, 1952. First shown Venice Film Festival, September 4th, 1953. 110 minutes.

French episode with: Jean-Pierre Mocky (Pierre), Etchika Choureau (Simone), Henri Poirier, André Jacques, Annie Noel, Guy de Meulan.

Italian episode with: Franco Interlenghi (Claudio), Anna-Maria Ferrero (Marina), Evi Maltagliati (Claudio's mother), Eduardo Cianelli (Claudio's father), Umberto Spadaro, Gastone Renzelli.

British episode with: Peter Reynolds (Aubrey), Fay Compton (Mrs Pinkerton), Patrick Barr (Kent Watton), Eileen Moore, Raymond Lovell, Derek Tansley, Jean Stuart, Tony Kilshaw, Fred Victor, Charles Irvin.

1953: LA SIGNORA SENZA CAMELIE
Production: ENIC (Domenico Forges Davanzati). Screenplay by Antonioni, Suso Cecchi D'Amico, Francesco Maselli, P. M. Pasinetti, from a story by Antonioni. Photographed by Enzo Serafin. Sets by Gianni Polidori. Music by Giovanni Fusco, played by Marcel Mule Saxophone Quintet. Assistant Director: Francesco Maselli. Director of production: Vittorio Glori. Shot in Rome, Venice, Milan, winter 1952-53. Première: Rome, February, 1953. 105 minutes.

With: Lucia Bosè (Clara Manni), Andrea Cecchi (Gianni Franchi), Gino Cervi (Ercole), Ivan Desny (Nardo Rusconi), Alain Cuny (Lodi), Monica Clay (Simonetta), Anna Carena (Clara's mother), Enrico Glori (Director), Laura Tiberti, Oscar Andriani, Elio Steiner, Nino Del Fabbro.

1953: TENTATO SUICIDIO (episode of AMORE IN CITTA)
Production: Faro Film. Story and Screenplay by Antonioni, Cesare Zavattini, Aldo Buzzi, Luigi Chiarini, Luigi Malerba, Tullio Pinelli, Vittorio Veltroni. Photographed by Gianni Di Venanzo. Sets by Gianni Polidori. Music by Mario Nascimbene. Edited by Eraldo Da Roma. Assistant Director: Luigi Vanzi. Production Director: Marco Ferreri. Shot in Rome. Première: Rome, November 27th, 1953. The first film inquiry sponsored by the film magazine Lo Spettatore run by Zavattini, Riccardo Ghione and Marco Ferreri. 20 minutes.

With the people who took part in the actual events reported in each episode.

1955: LE AMICHE—*The Girl Friends*
Production: Trionfalcine (Giovanni Addessi).Screenplay by Antonioni, Suso Cecchi D'Amico, Alba De Cespedes from a story *Tra Donne Sole*, in book *La Bella Estate* by Cesare Pavese. Photographed by Gianni Di Venanzo. Sets by Gianni Polidori. Costumes by the House of Fontana. Music by Giovanni Fusco; guitar played by Libero Tosoni; piano played by Armando Trovajoli. Edited by Eraldo Da Roma. Assistant Director: Luigi Vanzi. Director of Production: Pietro Notarianni. Shot in Turin. First shown at Venice Film Festival, September 7th, 1955. Première, Rome, November 18th, 1955. 104 minutes.

With: Eleanora Rossi Drago (Clelia), Valentina Cortese (Nene), Gabriele Ferzetti (Lorenzo), Franco Fabrizi (the architect, Cesare Pedoni), Ettore Manni (the architect's assistant, Carlo), Madeleine Fischer (Rosetta Savoni), Yvonne Furneaux (Momina De Stefani), Annamaria Pancani (Mariella), Maria Gambarelli (Clelia's employer), Luciano Volpato.

1957: IL GRIDO—*The Cry*
Production: S.P.A. Cinematografica (Franco Cancellieri) in collaboration with Robert Alexander Productions, New York. Screenplay by Antonioni, Ennio De Concini, Elio Bartolini from a story by Antonioni. Photographed by Gianni Di Venanzo. Sets by Franco Fontana. Costumes by Pia Marchesi. Music by Giovanni Fusco; piano played by Lya De Barberis. Edited by Eraldo Da Roma. Assistant Director: Luigi Vanzi. Director of Production: Danilo Marciano, Ralph Pinto. Shot in the Po valley, winter 1956-57. First shown at Locarno Film Festival, July 14th, 1957. Première: Rome, November 29th, 1957. 116 minutes.

With: Steve Cochran (Aldo), Alida Valli (Irma), Betsy Blair (Elvira), Dorian Gray (Virginia), Gabriella Pallotta (Edera), Lynn Shaw (Andreina), Mirna Girardi (Rosina), Gaetano Matteucci, Guerrino Campanili, Pina Boldrini.

1960: L'AVVENTURA
Production by Amato Penn, for Cino del Duca, Produzioni Cinematografiche Europèe (Rome), Société

Cinématographique Lyre (Paris). Screenplay by Antonioni, Elio Bartolini, Tonino Guerra from a story by Antonioni. Photographed by Aldo Scavarda. Sets by Piero Poletto. Costumes by Adriana Berselli. Music by Giovanni Fusco. Edited by Eraldo Da Roma. Assistant Director: Franco Indovina, Gianni Arduini. Director of Production: Luciano Perugia. Shot in Rome and Sicily (the Isles of Lipari, Milazzo, Catania, Taormina), September 1959 - January 1960. Première: Bologna, September 25th, 1960. 145 minutes.

With: Gabriele Ferzetti (Sandro), Monica Vitti (Claudia) Lea Massari (Anna), Dominique Blanchar (Giulia), Renzo Ricci (Anna's father), James Addams (Corrado), Dorothy De Poliolo (Gloria Perkins), Lelio Luttazzi (Raimondo), Giovanni Petrucci (young painter), Esmeralda Ruspoli (Patrizia), Joe, fisherman from Panarea (old man on the island), Prof. Cucco (Ettore), Enrico Bologna, Franco Cimino, Giovanni Danesi, Rita Molè, Renato Piciroli, Angela Tommasi Di Lampedusa, Vincenzo Tranchina.

1961: LA NOTTE—*The Night*

Production: by Emanuele Cassuto for Nepi-Film (Rome), Silva-Film (Rome), Sofitedip (Paris). Screenplay by Antonioni, Ennio Flaiano, Tonino Guerra from a story by Antonioni. Photographed by Gianni Di Venanzo. Sets by Piero Zuffi Costumes by Biki. Music by Giorgio Gaslini played by the Quartetto Giorgio Gaslini. Edited by Eraldo Da Roma. Assistant Directors: Franco Indovina, Berto Pelosso. Director of Production: Paolo Frascà. Shot in Milan, July, August 1960. Première: Milan, January 24th, 1961. 122 minutes.

With: Marcello Mastroianni (Giovanni Pontano), Jeanne Moreau (Lidia), Monica Vitti (Valentina Gherardini), Bernhard Wicki (Tommaso), Maria Pia Luzi (Patient), Rosy Mazzacurati (Resy), Guido A. Marsan (Fanti), Gitt Magrini (Signora Gherardini), Vincenzo Corbella (Gherardini), Giorgio Negro (Roberto), Roberta Speroni (Berenice), Ugo Fortunati (Cesarino), Vittorio Bertolini, Valentino Bompiani, Salvatore Quasimodo, Giansiro Ferrata, Roberto Danesi, Ottiero Ottieri.

1962: L'ECLISSE—*The Eclipse*

Production by Robert and Raymond Hakim for Interopa Film, Cineriz (Rome), Paris Film Production (Paris), Screenplay by Antonioni, Tonino Guerra, Elio Bartolini, Ottiero Ottieri from a story by Antonioni and Guerra. Photographed by Gianni Di Venanzo. Sets by Piero Poletto. Music by Giovanni Fusco; Eclisse Twist sung by Mina. Edited by Eraldo Da Roma. Assistant Director: Franco Indovina, Gianni Arduini. Director of Production: Danilo Marciano. Shot in Rome and Verona,

Autumn 1961. First shown: Cannes Film Festival, 1962 Première: Paris, August 1962. 125 minutes.

With: Monica Vitti (Vittoria), Alain Delon (Piero), Lilla Brignone (Vittoria's mother), Francisco Rabal (Riccardo), Louis Seignier (Ercoli), Rossana Rory (Anita), Mirella Ricciardi (Marta), Cyrus E's (drunk).

1964: DESERTO ROSSO—*Le Desert Rouge, The Red Desert*

Production by Antonio Cervi for Film Duemila, Cinematografica Federiz (Rome), Francoriz (Paris). Story and Screenplay by Antonioni and Tonino Guerra. Photographed by Carlo Di Palma in Technicolor. Sets by Piero Poletto. Costumes by Gitt Magrini. Music by Giovanni Fusco; sung by Cecilia Fusco; electronic music by Vittorio Gelmetti. Edited by Eraldo Da Roma. Assistant Directors: Giovanni Arduini, Flavio Nicolini. Director of Production: Ugo Tucci. Shot in Ravenna and Sardinia, October-December 1963. First shown: Venice Film Festival 1964. 120 minutes (U.K. 116 minutes).

With: Monica Vitti (Giuliana), Richard Harris (Corrado Zeller), Carlo Chionetti (Ugo), Xenia Valderi (Linda), Rita Renoir (Emilia), Aldo Grotti (Max), Giuliano Missirini (radio-telescope operator), Lili Rheims (his wife), Valerio Bartoleschi (son of Giuliana), Emanuela Paola Carboni (girl in the fable), Bruno Borghi, Beppe Conti, Giulio Cotignoli, Giovanni Lolli, Hiram Mino Madonia, Arturo Parmiani, Carla Ravasi, Ivo Cherpiani, Bruno Scipioni.

1965: PREFAZIONE (episode of I TRE VOLTI)

Production: Dino De Laurentiis. Story and Screenplay by Piero Tosi. Photographed by Carlo Di Palma. Sets and costumes by Piero Tosi. Music by Piero Piccioni. Edited by Eraldo Da Roma.

With Soraya, Ivano Davoli, Giorgio Sartarelli, Piero Tosi, Dino De Laurentiis, Alfredo De Laurentiis, Ralph Serpe (American producer).

1966: BLOW-UP

Production: Bridge Films (Carlo Ponti) for MGM. Executive producer: Pierre Rouve. Screenplay by Antonioni and Tonino Guerra from a short story by Julio Cortazar; English dialogue in collaboration with Edward Bond. Photography by Carlo Di Palma in Metrocolor. Sets by Assheton Gorton; photographic murals by John Cowan. Costumes by Jocelyn Rickards. Music by Herbert Hancock; 'Stroll On' featured by The Yardbirds. Edited by Frank Clarke. Assistant Director: Claude Watson. Director of Production: Donald Toms. Shot in London and at MGM studio, Boreham Wood. Première: New York, December 1966. 111 minutes.

With: Vanessa Redgrave (Jane), David Hemmings (Thomas), Sarah Miles (Patricia), Peter Bowles (Ron),

Verushka, Jill Kennington, Peggy Moffitt, Rosaleen Murray, Ann Norman, Melanie Hampshire (models), Jane Birkin, Gillian Hills (Teenagers), Harry Hutchinson (Antique dealer), John Castle (Painter).

1968: ZABRISKIE POINT
Produced by Carlo Ponti for MGM With Rod Taylor. Filming commenced Summer 1968 on location in Phoenix, Arizona, in Nevada and in Death Valley.

Other work
Credited as Technical Supervisor on *Questo nostro mondo* (1958) directed by Ugo Lazzari, Eros Macchi, Angelo Negri, but does not acknowledge working on the film. Worked as a producer on a short, *Uomini in più*, (1955) directed by Nicolò Ferrari for the Intergovernmental Committee on European Migration (C.I.M.E.). It was concerned with the problems of over-population and emigration in Italy. In 1957 he directed two plays at the Teatro Eliseo in Rome, 'Scandali segreti' (written with Elio Bartolini and based on an unfilmed scenario) and 'I am a Camera', with Monica Vitti. In 1958, he directed the second unit for Alberto Lattuada's *La Tempesta* and replaced Guido Brignone, who died during the retakes, as director on *Nel Segno di Roma*. During 1958, he also worked on another spectacular.

Unfilmed screenplays
Scale (1950)
Ida e i porci (1956) in collaboration with Ennio De Concini and Rodolfo Sonego.
Le allegre ragazze del 24 (1956), set in the 'twenties and to be shot in colour.
Uno dei 'nostri figli' (1952), originally intended to be the Italian episode of *I Vinti* but, because of censorship, never filmed. Written in collaboration with Giorgio Bassani and Suso Cecchi D'Amico.
Makaroni (1958), an adaptation written with Tonino Guerra of Ugo Pirro's novel *Le soldatesse*, which was later filmed under that title by Valerio Zurlini.

BIBLIOGRAPHY
Books about Antonioni
BERNARDINI, Aldo, *Michelangelo Antonioni da 'Gente del Po' a 'Blow-Up'*. Edizioni 17, Milan, 1967.
COWIE, Peter, *Antonioni, Bergman, Resnais*. The Tantivy Press, London, 1963.
CUENCA, Carlos Fernandez, *Michelangelo Antonioni*. Filmoteca Nacional de Espana, Madrid, 1963.
LEPROHON, Pierre, *Michelangelo Antonioni*. Cinéma d'Aujourd'hui 2, Pierre Seghers, Paris, 1961. English translation by Scott Sullivan, Simon & Schuster, New York, 1963.
RANIERI, Tino, *Michelangelo Antonioni*. Opusculo del CUC, Trieste, 1958.

STRICK, Philip, *Antonioni*. Motion Publications, Loughton, 1963.
TAILLEUR, Roger, and THIRARD, Paul-Louis, *Antonioni*. Editions Universitaires, Paris, 1963.
THIRARD, Paul-Louis, *M. A. Antonioni*. Premier Plan 15, SERDOC, Lyon, 1960.
TAYLOR, John Russell, in *Cinema Eye, Cinema Ear*. Methuen, London, 1964.
VOGLINO, Bruno, *Michelangelo Antonioni*. Centrofilm 3, Turin, 1959.

Film about Antonioni
MINGOZZI, Gianfranco (director), *Michelangelo Antonioni*, with commentary by Tommaso Chiaretti. 16mm., 61 minutes. IDI Cinematografica, 1965.

Scripts and outlines
The Screenplays of Michelangelo Antonioni, with an introduction by the author, including *Il Grido*, *L'Avventura*, *La Notte*, *L'Eclisse*. Orion Press, New York, 1963.
Sei film. As above plus *Le Amiche*, *Il Deserto Rosso*. Einaudi, Turin, 1964.
Il Grido, edited by Elio Bartolini, Cappelli, Bologna, 1957.
L'Avventura, edited by Tommaso Chiaretti, Cappelli, Bologna, 1960. French translation, Buchet-Chastel, Paris.
La Notte, Buchet-Chastel, Paris.
L'Eclisse, edited by John Francis Lane, Cappelli, Bologna, 1962.
Deserto Rosso, edited by Carlo Di Carlo, Cappelli, Bologna, 1964. French translation in L'Avant-Scène du Cinéma 49, Paris, 1965.
Blow-Up, Italian translation, Giulio Einaudi, Turin, 1968. Swedish translation, Norstedts, Stockholm, 1967.
Uno dei 'nostri figli', the banned Italian episode for *I Vinti*. Story, written in collaboration with Giorgio Bassani and Suso Cecchi D'Amico, in Cinema 138, 1954, reprinted in Voglino (op. cit.). French translation in Positif 39, Paris, 1961 and in Leprohon (op. cit.).
Le allegre ragazze del 24, story for a period film in colour, in Cinema Nuovo 85, Rome, 1956. French translation in Thirard (op. cit.).
Makaroni, project written in collaboration with Tonino Guerra, Cinema Nuovo 163-5, Rome 1963. French translation in Positif 66-67-68, Paris 1965.
La Noche, el Eclipse, el Desierto Rojo, Alianza Editorial, Madrid, 1967.
Blow-Up, las Amigas, el Grito, La Aventura, Alianza Editorial, Madrid, 1968.